ELEVATE

ELEVATE

THE **THREE DISCIPLINES** OF
ADVANCED STRATEGIC THINKING

RICH HORWATH

WILEY

Published by John Wiley & Sons, Inc., Hoboken, New Jersey.
Published simultaneously in Canada.

For general information about our other products and services, please contact our Customer Care Department within the United States at (800) 762-2974, outside the United States at (317) 572-3993 or fax (317) 572-4002.

Wiley publishes in a variety of print and electronic formats and by print-on-demand. Some material included with standard print versions of this book may not be included in e-books or in print-on-demand. If this book refers to media such as a CD or DVD that is not included in the version you purchased, you may download this material at http://booksupport.wiley.com. For more information about Wiley products, visit www.wiley.com.

Library of Congress Cataloging-in-Publication Data:

Horwath, Rich.
    Elevate : the three disciplines of advanced strategic thinking / Rich Horwath.
        pages   cm
    Includes bibliographical references and index.
    ISBN 978-1-118-59646-3 (cloth); ISBN 978-1-118-65324-1 (ebk);
    ISBN 978-1-118-65350-0 (ebk)
    1. Strategic planning.   I. Title.
  HD30.28.H682   2014
  658.4'012—dc23

                                                        2013046707

Printed in the United States of America
10 9 8 7 6 5 4 3 2 1

For my wife Anne, daughter Jessica, and son Luke,
who, at five years old, compared my CD on
strategy to a sermon at church:

"There's a lot of talking, I don't understand most of it,
and I think I'm getting sleepy."

CONTENTS

INTRODUCTION

Elevate

To see things in a new way,
we must rise above the fray.

Approaching the Hughes 269C helicopter, the first thing I notice are the doors—there aren't any. "Nope, no doors," explains Chris, my helicopter flight instructor. "Gets too hot in there." It's amazing how much more closely you pay attention to the seat belt instructions when the aircraft you're about to go up in has no doors. After completing a thorough pre-flight checklist of some 60 items, including a review of the helicopter's nose area, cabin, engine, main rotor system, tail boom, and tail rotor, we slip into the only two seats in the helicopter. Chris walks us through another review, this one being the 64 items on the pre-takeoff checklist and we're ready to go.

As we elevate into the clear blue sky, I'm immediately struck by how different things look from this vantage point, even though we're only about 500 feet up. I see patterns of traffic on the roads and the outlines of towns bumping up against one another. I see features of buildings I've not seen from this perspective. I see homes on 10- and 20-acre parcels of land, too secluded to see from the ground. Now, I see it all.

Then Chris says, "Ok, your turn to fly this thing." He reminds me how the cyclic stick—used to tilt the main rotor disc by changing the pitch angle of the rotor blades on top of the chopper—should be treated like a martini. Any big, jerky moves of the martini glass and your drink will spill. It's the same concept with the cyclic. It should be moved slightly and smoothly, as the tilting of the rotor disc in a particular direction results in the helicopter moving in that direction. At the same time, my feet are on the tail rotor pedals, which control the smaller blades at the back of the helicopter. Since we're in a hovering position, the tail rotor pedals are controlling the direction of the nose of the helicopter. I'm checking the flight instruments inside the helicopter and scanning the air space around us for other aircraft, buildings, and electrical lines.

"You know you just took us up 100 feet?" Chris asks.

"Uh, no," I answer, as a 20-knot wind blows through the open cabin. I feel the helicopter swaying and realize I just took us up another 100 feet. Anxiety growing and confidence shrinking, I say, "Maybe you should take the controls back."

"Sure," says Chris, smiling as he notices my left hand clinging to the underside of the seat as we bank right, my body tilting towards the opening where the door should be. I'm staring at the countryside below, and thinking, "Thank God I got the seatbelt part right." My helicopter piloting lesson had come to an end.

What I took away from the lesson is that it requires great knowledge, preparation, and skill to capably fly a helicopter. I obviously didn't have these things, but my instructor did. The mastery to operate multiple controls simultaneously, monitor the flight instruments (internal conditions), assess the air space (external conditions), and devise an intelligent flight plan all contribute to a successful journey. And so it is with leading a business. A truly strategic leader possesses the mastery to manage multiple initiatives simultaneously, monitor the internal conditions of the business (e.g., people, processes, culture, etc.), assess the external conditions (e.g., market trends, customer needs, competitive landscape, etc.), and design a strategic action plan to achieve the goals and objectives. In both cases, elevation is required.

To elevate means to lift up, or to raise to a higher rank or intellectual level.[1] A helicopter is arguably the most precise, agile vehicle for physically raising a person up to considerable heights. Unlike fixed-wing aircraft (planes), helicopters are able to hover in one position for extended periods of time, ranging from a few feet above the ground to more than 36,000 feet high. One of the biggest challenges I continually hear from CEOs and talent management leaders is, "We need to elevate our manager's thinking." In essence, they're saying that managers need to be able to quickly elevate their thinking from down in the tactical weeds of day-to-day operations to a higher level. At this higher level, they can expand their perspective to understand how the core foundational elements of their business fit together and provide superior value to customers. The challenge of taking time to elevate one's thinking is supported by an Economist Intelligence Unit survey in which 64 percent of managers in bottom-performing companies cited the challenge: "We are too busy fighting the daily battles to step back."[2]

A helicopter has the agility to navigate within congested areas, such as skyscraper-filled cities, and also get to remote areas not accessible by any other means, such as mountaintops, giving them unmatched versatility. This versatility translates into a variety of functions ranging from emergency medical transport to aerial attacks by military forces. As author James Chiles wrote, "Of all birds, winged mammals and insects, very few have mastered the skill of pausing in midair and going backward as well as forward, so anything capable of such flight is a rare beast."[3] Business leaders also require agility—mental agility. Mental agility enables leaders to think clearly through the congestion of information—which comes in the form of e-mails, reports, and meetings—to isolate the trade-offs and decisions that will make or break their success. In both cases, a fair amount of risk is assumed.

Importance of Strategy

The inability to elevate thinking in order to set strategic direction can have devastating long-term effects on an organization. Research by The Conference Board has shown that 70 percent of public companies experiencing a revenue stall lose more than half of their market capitalization.[4] Additional research attributes the primary cause of these revenue stalls to poor decisions about strategy.[5] While it's convenient to blame an organization's failings on external factors such as the economy, decisions about strategy account for failure a whopping 70 percent of the time.[6] Following are two examples of executives citing external factors, in these cases "headwinds," for their organizations' failings:

We faced a number of competitive headwinds that became more pronounced in the second quarter.[7]

—Telecom CFO

We are saddened by this development. We were all working hard towards a different outcome, but the headwinds we have been facing for quite some time . . . have brought us to where we are now [bankruptcy].[8]

—Retail store president

So, the next time you hear someone blaming the economy or headwinds for their poor performance, smile and hand them a mirror. If you're going to take credit when things go well, then you'll need to take accountability when things don't go well. And that accountability begins with your strategy. As former United States Treasury Secretary Paul O'Neill said, "The great companies don't make excuses, including excuses about how they didn't do well because the economy was against them or prices were not good. They do well anyway."[9]

When poor decisions about strategy are made and an organization goes through a revenue stall, it's been shown that, on average, low performance continues for more than 10 years.[10] Unfortunately, this prolonged period of poor performance can lead to bankruptcy. Research on 750 bankruptcies during a 25-year period showed that the number-one factor behind these bankruptcies was bad strategy.[11] Contrary to popular opinion, the researchers attributed the failures to *flaws in the strategies themselves*, not to *poor execution* of the strategies. Therefore, it's important to be skilled at crafting strategy.

Great strategy is created by great strategists. Great strategy doesn't magically emerge from Excel spreadsheets, or elaborate PowerPoint decks. It comes from managers who can think strategically. In the *Wall*

Street Journal, Filippo Passerini, president of global business services and CIO at Procter & Gamble asserts:

> *It is becoming even more important to have the right strategies in place at the right point in time. Having the right strategies now is so important because if you happen to be wrong, you will derail within months. In the past, to figure out you were wrong, would take a few years. Now in three to six months, you may be in grave difficulty if you don't have the right strategies.*[12]

While most managers believe strategy is an inherent factor in their organization's success, several studies also document the support for this claim. One study concludes that, "strategy has a positive and significant effect on a firm's performance. Specifically, it is found to influence both the growth and profitability of a firm."[13] Another study summarized its findings as, "strategy contributes to profitability differences between successful and unsuccessful companies."[14] While both anecdotal and empirical evidence demonstrate the importance of strategy to an organization's success and the lack of strategy to an organization's failure, a thoughtful, methodical, and practical approach to strategy development is not common. A survey of more than 2,000 global executives found that only 19 percent of managers said that their companies have a distinct process for developing strategy.[15] For those firms that do have a process for strategy development, an alarming 67 percent of managers said that their organization is bad at developing strategy.[16] Clearly, there are some real-world challenges managers face in bridging the "knowing-doing gap" when it comes to strategy. Most managers know it's important, but few do it effectively.

Top 10 Strategy Challenges

During the past decade, while leading strategic thinking workshops around the world, I've recorded a list of nearly 40 challenges that managers have said prevent them from effectively developing, communicating, and executing strategy. Honing my study down to 25 companies and the responses of more than 500 managers, the top 10 strategy challenges and the frequency of each challenge by company are listed in Table I.1.

Table I.1   Strategy Challenges

Challenge	Percentage of Organizations
1. Time	96
2. Commitment (buy-in)	72
3. Lack of priorities	60
4. Status quo	56
5. Not understanding what strategy is	48
6. Lack of training/tools for thinking strategically	48
7. Lack of alignment	48
8. Firefighting (being reactive)	44
9. Lack of quality/timely data and information	36
10. Unclear company direction	32

1. **Time (96 percent).** The most commonly cited strategy challenge is time. With more responsibilities and fewer people to handle them, many managers are overwhelmed with activities. While checking lots of tasks off a to-do list each week may foster a sense of accomplishment, activity doesn't always equal achievement. If the individual tasks aren't strongly supporting the strategy, then we may fall into the trap of activity for activity's sake. When there are lots of things to do, managers feel guilty stopping to take time to think strategically about the business. After all, most performance reviews don't include a big box for "Thinks strategically for six hours a week," with the rating of "Exceeds Expectations," marked in it. When there is a lot to get done, time to think is often the first thing to go.

2. **Commitment (72 percent).** Gaining commitment from others to support and execute the strategy vexes many managers. Often referred to as *buy-in*, commitment can be challenging for several reasons. If the people expected to execute the strategy aren't aware of it, or don't understand it, then commitment will be non-existent. According to a study out of Harvard Business

School, a shocking 95 percent of employees in large organizations are either unaware of or don't understand their company strategies.[17] This finding may be rejected out of hand by some senior leaders, but it's crucial to find out just how high that percentage is for your group. Another reason buy-in is lacking is because many people don't understand the reasons behind the strategy and how it will help them achieve their goals. A study of 23,000 workers found that only 20 percent said they understood how their tasks relate to the organization's goals and strategies.[18] If leaders fail to share why the strategies are in place, and don't translate them to people's respective work, the level of commitment will be minimal.

3. **Lack of priorities (60 percent).** A great cause of frustration among managers is the overall lack of priorities at the leadership level. When everything is deemed important, it creates an overflowing-plate syndrome. If clear priorities are not established up front, then it becomes difficult for people to determine what they should be working on and why. This lack of priorities prevents people from taking things off of their plate, resulting in the frustration of feeling spread too thin by too many initiatives. A lack of priorities is a red flag that the difficult work of making trade-offs—choosing some things and not others—was not accomplished in setting the strategy. Good strategy requires trade-offs, which in turn help establish priorities by filtering out activities that don't contribute to the achievement of goals.

4. **Status quo (56 percent).** Numerous studies in the social sciences have shown that people prefer the status quo to change.[19] When people change strategy, inevitably they are changing the allocation of resources, including how people invest their time, talent, and budgets. Since strategy involves trade-offs, certain people will be gaining resources and others losing resources. Obviously, those slated to lose resources are going to prefer to keep things they way they are. Another factor in the preference of the status quo is the "if it ain't broke, don't fix it," mentality. For groups that have experienced success in the past, the idea

of making changes to the strategy flies in the face of common sense, so their question is, "Why change what made us successful?" What they may not realize is that changes in market trends, customer value drivers, and the competitive landscape may be making the current strategy obsolete. In leading a revival at Starbucks during his second stint as CEO, Howard Schultz said, "We cannot be content with the status quo. Any business today that embraces the status quo as an operating principle is going to be on a death march."[20]

5. **Not understanding what strategy is (48 percent).** Even at the highest levels of organizations, confusion abounds as to what exactly is a strategy. Perhaps due to its abstract nature, strategy tends to mean different things to different people. It's often confused with mission, vision, goals, objectives, and even tactics. Failure to provide managers with a universal definition of strategy, and clear examples to refer to, leaves the term open to interpretation, creating ineffective plans and inefficient communication. To determine the level of understanding in your group, provide each manager with a 3" × 5" notecard at your next meeting and ask each person to record their definition of strategy along with an example. Collect the cards, read them aloud to the group, and tally the number that defined strategy in the same way. Professor Richard Rumelt describes the problem this way: "Too many organizational leaders say they have a strategy when they do not. . . . A long list of things to do, often mislabeled as strategies or objectives, is not a strategy. It is just a list of things to do."[21]

6. **Lack of training/tools for thinking strategically (48 percent).** Many managers aren't considered strategic simply because they've never been educated on what it means to think and act strategically. For many years in the pharmaceutical industry, district sales managers were not asked to be strategic, because the blockbuster business model combined with the reach and frequency sales approach proved to be a winning formula. However, changes in the industry—including healthcare

reform, geographic differences in managed care, reimbursement policies, and the emergence of Accountable Care Organizations (ACOs)—now require district sales managers to strategically allocate their resources and make trade-offs between different opportunities to grow their business. Research has found that 90 percent of directors and vice presidents have received no training to become competent business strategists.[22] It shouldn't be a shock then that a Harris Interactive study with 154 companies found only 30 percent of managers to be strategic thinkers.[23] The disconnect on proficiency in strategic thinking can sometimes occur between a CEO's perspective and the perspective of senior executives. A global survey showed that while only 28 percent of CEOs felt their teams needed improvement in strategic thinking, more than half of the non-CEO executives indicated that strategic thinking skills were in need of improvement.[24] Procter & Gamble CEO A. G. Lafley writes, "There simply is no one perfect strategy that will last for all time. There are multiple ways to win in almost any industry. That's why building up strategic thinking capability within your organization is so vital."[25]

7. **Lack of alignment (48 percent).** Getting people on the proverbial same page is difficult when it comes to strategy. The challenge lies in the fact that different groups within the organization have their own goals and strategies. Sometimes they align with others, but often times they don't. When there is misalignment, power struggles erupt and instead of working with one another, managers from different areas work against each other to ensure their priorities take precedence. Lack of alignment can also occur between executive teams and the organization's board of directors. Some organizations use their board to provide input into the development of strategy and some use the board to review the already completed strategy in a Q&A-format presentation. Selecting the optimal intellectual exchange and setting appropriate expectations for contribution can be critical to a CEO's success. A survey of 1,000 corporate directors found

the number-one reason for success and the number-one reason for failure in CEO appointments dealt with strategic alignment between the CEO and the board.[26]

8. **Firefighting (44 percent).** Make no mistake, a firefighting mentality starts at the top of the organization. If managers see their senior leaders constantly reacting to every issue that comes across their desk, they too will adopt this behavior. Firefighting then becomes embedded in the culture and those that are seen as the most reactive, oddly enough, garner the greatest recognition. Managers who thoughtfully consider each issue before responding don't seem to be doing as much as the firefighters, when in reality, they're exponentially more productive.

"Let's think about that," is a simple but powerful phrase that can eliminate reactivity within your business and culture. The next time you receive an e-mail marked urgent or someone comes charging into your office with how to react to a competitor's activity or a new flavor-of-the-month project, reply with "Let's think about that." Then stop and consider how this helps you achieve your goals and supports your strategic focus. To do so, determine the probability of success, impact on the business, and resources required. If after this analysis, the new task doesn't appear to support your goals and strategies, kindly inform the relevant parties that, relative to the other initiatives you're working on, this doesn't warrant resource allocation.

9. **Lack of quality/timely data and information (36 percent).** Strategic thinking is defined as the ability to generate new insights on a continual basis to achieve competitive advantage. An insight is the combination of two or more pieces of information or data in a unique way that leads to the creation of new value. So, at the core of strategic thinking is the information or data, which we piece together in unique ways to come up with new approaches, new methods, or new solutions for providing superior value to customers. Managers who aren't receiving timely, high-quality information and data regarding the key aspects of their business are going to be

hindered in their ability to think strategically—and the ability to understand this information is critical. A study showed that 62 percent of workers cannot make sense of the data that they receive.[27] Without clear priorities and methods for understanding, categorizing, and sharing insights, managers at all levels will continue to struggle with generating new ways to achieve their goals and objectives. Research by the consultancy McKinsey & Company verified the challenge managers face when it comes to profitably growing their business on strategic insights:

A fresh strategic insight—something your company sees that no one else does—is one of the foundations of competitive advantage. It helps companies focus their resources on moves that separate them from the pack. Only 35 percent of 2,135 global executives believed their strategies rested on unique and powerful insights.[28]

10. **Unclear company direction (32 percent).** It's difficult for managers to set strategy if there isn't clear strategic direction at the business unit and corporate levels. In some organizations, there are strategies at the business unit and corporate levels, but they're kept secret. Evidently, this secrecy is to prevent competitors from finding out their strategy. While it's understandable to keep proprietary processes and future intellectual properties secret, it makes little sense to keep strategy hidden away. If strategy is how to achieve the goals and objectives, it's impossible to gain full engagement and proper commitment from employees in rolling out the strategy if they don't know what it is. The other main reasons for unclear company direction are lack of process to develop strategy, a "we're too busy to plan" approach, and ignorance as to what comprises sound strategy. Managers from more than 500 companies have taken an assessment I developed called, "Is Your Organization Strategic?" and the average score is 45 percent, a failing grade, indicating there are many rudderless companies out there that are strategically adrift.

GOST Framework

At the heart of most strategy challenges is a lack of clarity as to what strategy is and how it differs from some of the other key business-planning terms. If you think that this lack of strategy knowledge only plagues new managers at the lower levels of the organization, take a look at the following quotations I've collected during my work from CEOs describing so-called strategies that aren't strategies at all:

- Become the global leader in our industry.
- Use innovation to build customer-centric solutions.
- Grow our audience.
- Strengthen core business, execute new initiatives, and reduce costs.
- Increase sales 25 percent in emerging markets by pursuing new growth opportunities.

The examples demonstrate how frequently the terms *goals*, *objectives*, *strategies*, and *tactics* are used interchangeably. I developed a simple framework called GOST (Figure I.1) to help managers at all levels use and teach others to use these business-planning terms appropriately.

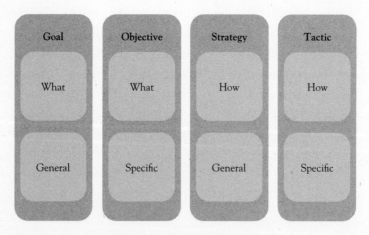

Figure I.1   GOST Framework

A goal is a target. It describes what you are trying to achieve in *general* terms. The following is an example of a goal for a regional sales director:

Goal: Win the national sales contest for our region.

An objective also describes what you are trying to achieve. The difference is, an objective is what you are trying to achieve in *specific* terms. The common acronym used to help flesh out an objective is SMART: specific, measurable, achievable, relevant, and time-bound. Objectives should meet these criteria, and they should flow directly from the goals you've already set. As evidenced in the following example, the objective matches up with the corresponding goal established earlier:

Goal: Win the national sales contest for our region.

Objective: Achieve $25 million in sales by the end of the third quarter of this year.

Once we've identified the goals and objectives, then we can determine the strategy, which is the path to achieving them. Strategy and tactics are *how* you will achieve your goals and objectives, how you will allocate your resources to succeed. Strategy is the *general* resource allocation plan. The tactics are *specifically* how you will do that. Using the previous example, we can see how the strategy serves as the path to achieving our goals and objectives.

Goal: Win the national sales contest for our region.

Objective: Achieve $25 million in sales by the end of the third quarter of this year.

Strategy: Focus selling efforts on expanding share of wallet with current customers.

Tactics: Have district sales managers work with sales reps to schedule appointments with the top five customers for each territory. Prepare a sell sheet showing dollarized value of using our products in combination. Videotape three customers using two or more of our products in combination. Purchase iPads and put new sell sheets and videos into a presentation for use during customer meetings. Create a dollarized, value-close, talking-points checklist to assist district managers and reps in expanding share of wallet.

If your managers are having trouble differentiating between strategy and tactics, they can use the "rule of touch." If you can reach out and physically touch it (e.g., sell sheet, training DVD, etc.), it's a tactic. The concept of strategy originated in the military arena thousands of years ago. Even that far back, Chinese general and philosopher Sun Tzu said, "All the men can see the tactics I use to conquer, but what none can see is the strategy out of which great victory is evolved."[29]

It's often said that strategy is long-term and tactics are short-term. In reality, long-term and short-term descriptors for strategy and tactics may or may not apply. A strategy that successfully helps you achieve your goal within three months might be short-term compared to tactics used for years to come in fending off a tough competitor. Using time as the criterion for distinguishing between strategy and tactics is common, but misinformed.

Since we can't see or physically reach out and touch strategy, it's often skipped in favor of going straight to tactics. A good number of the business plans I've reviewed over the past 15 years list goals, objectives, and tactics, skipping strategy all together. If strategy is not determined before tactics, there is no way of intelligently changing course when objectives and their corresponding milestones are not being achieved. Having a high-performance car (tactic) doesn't help you reach the other side of the river if there isn't a bridge (strategy) to cross it. With no strategy in place, it's easy to fall into a game of tactical roulette, where you continually chamber a new tactic and pull the trigger, hoping something hits its target. But, sooner or later, you'll be looking at a dead plan.

Strategy Defined

Strategy can be fully defined as the intelligent allocation of limited resources through a unique system of activities to outperform the competition in serving customers. Resources include time, talent, and capital. To provide the opportunity to sustain success, it's helpful to build strategy around multiple activities that either are different from the competition, or can be performed in different ways than the competition. For companies in mature markets, activities such as direct sales, manufacturing, and supply chain management are most likely similar across the industry. However, finding unique ways to perform these activities is where new value is created for customers. While digital networks for job searches have existed for quite some time, LinkedIn has been able to create a virtual professional network for job seekers and recruiters that has also transformed into a content hub. LinkedIn now receives content from 1.5 million publishers in order to provide new value for its nearly 250 million members.[30] They've taken a common activity, supporting job searches, and built different ways of doing it, adding new layers of value for their customers.

The idea of uniqueness—performing different activities or performing similar activities differently than the competition—is at the core of strategy. Unfortunately, it's easier said than done. A survey of more than 4,000 executives found that the number-one business challenge they faced was achieving competitive differentiation.[31] It's common for managers to look at their mature market and surrender to the notion that there are no differences between their offerings and those of the competition. They become resigned to battling it out with competitors on price, which rarely turns out well. A study of more than 25,000 companies found that the companies achieving the greatest return on assets (ROA) over an extended period of time employed differentiation rather than purely low prices. Researchers Michael Raynor and Mumtaz Ahmed summarized their findings by reporting: "Competitive positions built on greater differentiation through brand, style, or reliability are more likely to drive exceptional performance than positions built on lower prices."[32] Starbuck's CEO Howard Schultz describes the differentiation challenge from his perspective: "Whether you are a high tech company or a coffee company, your responsibility has to be to constantly create the kind of excitement that provides differentiation and separation in the marketplace."[33] When we discuss competitive advantage in the "Compete" section, you will find additional insights into how to create differentiated value using practical tools to hone your thinking in this crucial area.

Thinking Strategically

The business you lead is built on an idea. In the turbulence of daily work filled with product specifications, customer initiatives, board of director meetings, and hundreds of other items, it's easy to lose sight of that idea. The idea started in someone's mind, maybe even yours. Over the years, the idea transformed into offerings in the form of products, services, experiences, and so on that a group of potential customers found valuable and were willing to pay for. Cash flow, receivables, intellectual property, brands, careers—everything flows from the idea.

Numbed by the analgesic of activity, we lose our ability to generate ideas. Less than half of managers believe that they are highly effective at generating new ideas.[34] The degeneration of one's ability to think strategically and generate new insights limits both individual and organizational progress. In a 10-year study of leaders at 35 organizations, the primary problem attributed to a lack of success was strategic thinking. One of the participants commented: "Our senior executives tend to get carried away by details and lose their strategic perspective. It is a major challenge to get our decision makers to think in strategic rather than operational terms."[35] Just because someone has a senior-level title on their business card doesn't automatically qualify them as an effective strategic thinker. Similarly, just because someone is a new entry-level manager, don't assume they can't contribute valuable insights that can potentially shape the organization's strategies.

The lack of strategic thinking in the workplace runs counter to what employers are looking for in managers. Two separate studies on the abilities organizations most desire in their leaders both found that the number-one, most sought after skill is strategic thinking.[36,37] With changes in the market, customer needs and the competitive landscape happening faster and faster, organizations seek managers that can quickly identify strategic insights and transform those insights into strategies that create differentiated value for customers. Managers that simply call out problems without thoughtfully providing a range of solutions are rapidly losing their luster. Their lack of effective contribution can no longer be hidden in organizations that have a reduced head count. My survey on strategic thinking knowledge with 1,160 managers shows an average score of 70 percent. On most grading scales, 70 percent is a C–. That certainly leaves significant room for improvement for those with the hunger to get better. Authors Michael Birshan and Jayanti Kar share their conclusion when they write, "We are entering the age of the strategist. Rare is the company, though, where all members of the top team have well-developed strategic muscles."[38]

To help managers move from being purely tactical to more strategic, I introduced the three basic disciplines of strategic thinking in my previous book, *Deep Dive: The Proven Method for Building Strategy, Focusing Your Resources, and Taking Smart Action*. The *three basic disciplines of strategic thinking* are as follows:

1. **Acumen**, which helps you generate key business insights
2. **Allocation**, which focuses resources through trade-offs
3. **Action**, which requires executing strategy to achieve goals

Using this simple framework, managers are equipped with a method to think strategically on a daily basis, not just annually during the strategic planning process. In practice, a manager could use these three disciplines in their daily interactions by asking questions like:

- What is my key insight from this meeting?
- Based on the strategy to achieve my goals, what are the trade-offs I need to make with my time, talent, and budget?
- Am I working on an activity that is important to execution of the strategy, or is it an urgent, but unimportant issue that's taken me off plan?

The three basic disciplines of acumen, allocation, and action include dozens of practical strategic thinking tools and questions to help managers strategically guide their business. Through training tens of thousands of managers on this framework, it has been rewarding to see the average manager's knowledge of strategic thinking increase by 30 percent within completion of the program. As these managers continued to hone the basic disciplines of strategic thinking and their responsibilities increased, the natural question for many was, "What's next? How can I best prepare myself to excel as a senior leader and become an elite strategist?"

Real-world leaders echoed this need. Indra Nooyi, CEO of Pepsi said, "To me, the single most important skill needed for any CEO today is strategic acuity."[39] USA Today asked David Novak, CEO of Yum Brands, parent company of KFC, Pizza Hut, and Taco Bell, "What's the key to being a successful global company?" He responded, "You need to be strategic."[40] And the Corporate Board of Directors Survey showed that the number-one trait of active CEOs that make them attractive board candidates is strategic expertise.[41]

Functional leaders in areas such as sales, marketing, finance, human resources, information technology, and operations bring great technical expertise to their roles. However, their technical expertise becomes an ante when they are given broader leadership responsibilities. Ascending to a general management position such as chief marketing officer, chief information officer, or chief learning officer now requires the ability to look at the business holistically. It demands trading in a functional perspective for a systemic one in which the leader can synthesize insights into tangible value for both internal and external customers. In an article entitled "The New Path to the C-Suite," Harvard Business School professor Boris Groysberg presented his research findings on what is required of leaders to succeed at the highest levels of the organization. Professor Groysberg summarized the results by writing:

> For the senior-most executives, functional and technical expertise has become less important than understanding business fundamentals and strategy. . . . One theme that ran through our findings was [that] the requirements for all the C-level jobs have shifted toward business acumen. To thrive as a C-level executive, an individual needs to be a good communicator, a collaborator, and a strategic thinker.[42]

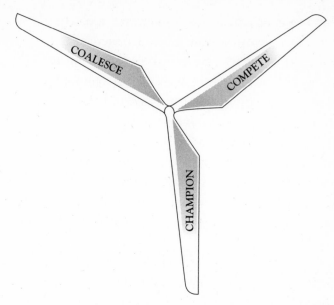

Figure I.2 The Three Disciplines of Advanced Strategic Thinking

To enable managers to elevate their thinking to a level that allows them to see the foundational elements of the business from a higher, more holistic vantage point, I've developed a framework called the *three disciplines of advanced strategic thinking* (Figure I.2):

1. **Coalesce:** Fusing together insights to create an innovative business model

2. **Compete:** Creating a system of strategy to achieve competitive advantage

3. **Champion:** Leading others to think and act strategically to execute strategy

The three disciplines of advanced strategic thinking provide leaders with new concepts to change mindsets and practical tools to enhance behaviors so that they are maximizing their strategic leadership potential. The fact that the framework elements are referred to as "disciplines" means that it takes time, effort, and commitment to master

them. In our action-oriented world, where we're electronically teth-
ered to one another, investing time to think on a regular basis can be a
challenge in itself. While it's easy to be pulled into one more meeting
that you really don't need to be in and check e-mail for the 47th time
today while meeting with others, this lack of discipline is going to
chain you to mediocrity. The adrenaline rush that comes from scram-
bling to fight another urgent, but unimportant fire, is addicting and
much more exciting than spending 30 quiet minutes thinking about
the business. But, it's these types of decisions that create your patterns
of thinking and behavior. It's the discipline, or lack of discipline, that
can make or break your career and determine the success or failure of
your business.

The "30,000 foot view" of the business is a common phrase used
to describe getting to a high enough level to see the big picture. The
next time you're in a commercial airplane and cruising around 30,000
feet, take a look out the window and note what you see—some clouds,
large swaths of land, maybe a mountain range. The reality is you're too
high up to see much of anything with any precision. Take a helicopter between 500 to 1,000 feet and you'll be able to clearly recognize
what you're looking at, with the benefit of seeing it from a new, higher
perspective. Buildings, homes, bridges, and roads are seen in a more
revealing way because of the elevation, while important details are still
clear to the eye. To reinforce your learning throughout the book, the
end of each section will include a summary of the key points called
the *1,000-Foot View*.

So, buckle up and prepare to elevate your thinking.

1,000-Foot View

The Top 10 Strategy Challenges Facing Managers
1. Time
2. Commitment
3. Lack of priorities
4. Status quo
5. Not understanding what strategy is
6. Lack of training/tools for thinking strategically
7. Lack of alignment
8. Firefighting
9. Lack of quality/timely data and information
10. Unclear company direction

GOST Framework
Goal: What to achieve (general)
Objective: What to achieve (specific)
Strategy: How to achieve (general)
Tactics: How to achieve (specific)

Strategy is the intelligent allocation of limited resources through a unique system of activity to outperform the competition in serving customers.

The Three Disciplines of Basic Strategic Thinking
1. **Acumen,** which helps you generate key business insights
2. **Allocation,** which focuses resources through trade-offs
3. **Action,** which requires executing strategy to achieve goals

The Three Disciplines of Advanced *Strategic Thinking*

1. **Coalesce:** Fusing together insights to create an innovative business model

2. **Compete:** Creating a system of strategy to achieve competitive advantage

3. **Champion:** Leading others to think and act strategically to execute strategy

Coalesce

*To bring together from disparate parts,
requires both the sciences and the arts.*

In January 1922 at the Royal Theater in Madrid, Juan de la Cierva watched a performance of *Don Quixote*. During the performance, Cierva's attention was drawn to a windmill on stage. He observed that the blades of the windmill flapped slightly with each rotation because they were made of flexible slivers of palm-tree wood. Cierva had been working on flight machine prototypes with blades atop the fuselage, and he had run up against one big problem: The propeller blades rolled to the right during testing. His revelation during *Don Quixote* was that the prototypes featured blades that couldn't flap, limiting the aircraft to a slow forward hover, which caused the roll over. If instead the blades were made of material that allowed them to flap like the windmill, then the advancing blade could flap upward, providing some lift, while the retreating blade flapped downward, producing extra lift. Cierva's flash of insight would prove to be the key principle in the flight of all single-main-rotor helicopters today.[1]

Cierva's discovery captures the essence of insight. An insight is the combination of two or more pieces of information or data in a unique way that leads to the creation of new value. Strategic thinking, then, is the ability to generate insights that lead to competitive advantage. Using the lens of *new value* on the ideas, projects, initiatives, and tactics proposed each day provides a powerful filter for eliminating meaningless activities. It forces you to more closely examine *why* things are being proposed and pursued instead of just *what* is to be done.

Advanced strategic thinking requires not only the insights generated, but the ability to coalesce these insights into meaningful differentiated value. Coalesce means to bring together, and we see this skill evident in great strategies and the strategists who have devised them. Steve Jobs's coalescing of insights from the computer, music, and telecommunications industries provided Apple much more than a single product hit. It provided Apple with the means to fuse design, integration, and convenience into a profit-chomping platform of products wrapped in a premium brand.

Strategy is often described as the big picture. Remember back to the connect-the-dots pages of your youth. Black dots were distributed throughout a page, each next to a number. By tracing a pencil in numerical order over the dots, you would create a picture. The more dots you connected, the more fully the picture would emerge. Prior to developing a strategy, the insights (black dots) must be generated and then connected in a meaningful sequence. The result is a holistic view of the current business situation and the path to achieve one's goals and objectives. Moving forward, we'll examine a number of different concepts and tools to enhance your ability to coalesce insights into cogent strategy.

Patterns in Strategy

A pattern is "a reliable sample of traits, acts, tendencies, or other observable characteristics of a person, group, or institution" as well as "a discernable coherent system based on the intended interrelationship of component parts."[2] Meteorologists attempt to map weather patterns, Major League Baseball pitchers attempt to identify batters' hitting patterns, and chess players use patterns to understand their opponents' plan of attack. Many of the technological advances we take for granted today including magnetic resonance imaging (MRIs), speech recognition software, and DNA sequencing analysis are based on the principle of pattern recognition. Every day, we communicate using specific combinations of letters and sounds, or patterns, to get our messages across.

From a business perspective, intended and unintended patterns are all around us. An intended pattern may be the human resource department's hiring process that creates a company comprised of a consistent type of employee with certain experience and skill sets. An unintended pattern may emerge when your sales team offers an end-of-the-year discount in a last-ditch effort to hit their numbers. The unintended aspect of this pattern is that customers now hold their orders until the fourth quarter to receive the discount, which in turn delays cash flow and lowers your profit margins.

Strategy has been characterized as ". . . the pattern of decisions in a company that determines and reveals its objectives, purposes, or goals. . . ."[3] This description makes practical sense as strategy is defined as *how* one goes about achieving their goals and objectives. The patterns of decisions your managers make regarding their strategic direction will ideally lead to the achievement of their goals and objectives. In his seminal 1971 book, *The Concept of Corporate Strategy*, former Harvard Business School professor Kenneth Andrews elaborates:

> *The pattern resulting from a series of strategic decisions will probably define the central character and image of the company. The pattern will permit the specification of particular objectives to be attained through a timed sequence of investment and implementation decisions and will govern directly the deployment or redeployment of resources to make these decisions effective.*[4]

As strategy involves the intelligent allocation of limited resources, it's imperative that positive patterns emerge in how those resources are allocated, and just as important, reallocated. A study of more than 200 large companies found that the *reallocation* of resources to faster-growing segments within a company's portfolio of businesses was the largest single driver of revenue growth.[5] Unfortunately, in many organizations the reallocation of resources generally happens only once a year, during the annual strategic planning process. Even then, how significant are the resource allocation shifts? While managers may tweak the tactics, the thoughtful redistribution of time, people, and budget from one initiative or area to another is rare. Examine your business plan from two years ago and compare it with this year's plan. How much difference is there between the two plans? If the answer is "not much," consider the results of another study on the effect of reallocation that demonstrates the potential size of this missed opportunity. McKinsey tracked firms' resource allocation over a 15-year period. They found that, regardless of the industry, the firms that reallocated the most resources (on average more than 50 percent of capital) across divisions produced shareholder returns that were about 30 percent higher than those companies that reallocated the least.[6]

For many managers, resources stuck in dead-end projects and unproductive tactics simply stay there until the next planning process rolls around. Sometimes it's politically dangerous to pull the plug on a lame-duck initiative, and sometimes it can be perceived that a mistake was made. No matter the cause, the strategic thinking trap of the sunk-cost effect—continuing to invest in a losing endeavor because resources have already been spent on it—can put an anvil around the effort to elevate thinking. The results can be damaging not only for companies, but also for their individual leaders. A study of CEOs with an average tenure of six years showed that those who reallocated resources the least during their first three years as CEO were much more likely to be fired in years four through six than those who reallocated more often.[7]

One clear indication of a lack of strategy is a random and pattern-less hodgepodge of decisions with no consistency in approach. Leaders who describe their strategic approach as *opportunistic* believe that every opportunity is considered a good one. These opportunistic leaders fail to create a disciplined pattern of focus on providing maximum value to the right type of customer. If you've ever felt like a bumper car bouncing randomly from one opportunity or project to the next with no real direction, then you understand the effect of a pattern-less approach to business. Advanced strategic thinkers recognize this pitfall and employ a pattern lens to their daily work. As Columbia Business School professor Rita McGrath notes, "Today's gifted strategists examine the data, certainly, but they also use advanced pattern recognition, direct observation and the interpretation of weak signals in the environment to set broad themes."[8]

Developing strong patterns of regular resource allocation should not be left to chance. As the research demonstrates, consistent patterns of productive allocation and reallocation are important barometers for long-term company and individual success. Andreas Kramvis, CEO of

Honeywell Performance Materials and Technologies, offers some practical guidelines:

> *To ensure that your organization is constantly reallocating resources
> from weak areas to promising ones, you need a systematic operating
> method. Most companies have a rhythm of meetings and performance
> reviews but spend much of their time looking in the rearview mirror:
> What was last month's performance? What was last year's perfor-
> mance? I believe you need to impose an operating mechanism that
> reallocates resources in real time and that educates your organization
> and instills core capabilities.*[9]

Inherent to identifying patterns in the marketplace and within
the customer and competitor arenas is the ability to understand the
current business context. While most managers focus their attention
using a functional (e.g., marketing) or geographic (e.g., Northeast
region) perspective, there's a need to look at the business from a
holistic point of view if we're to spot relevant patterns. As patterns
develop over time, it's important to be continually monitoring the
business to detect their emergence. One method of pattern detection
is to examine snapshots of the business at different points in time to
identify combinations of activities or tendencies. To do so, a series
of Contextual Radars can be created on a periodic basis and then
examined for patterns.

Radar is a method of detecting objects and determining their positions, velocities, or other characteristics using high-frequency radio
waves reflected from their surfaces. In a similar fashion, the Contextual
Radar provides a visual snapshot of the four primary components of
business: market, customers, competitors, and the company. At the
center of the radar are any issues or activities that are at the core of
changes in the business.

Figures 1.1 through 1.3 show highlights of the Contextual Radar
completed for three consecutive quarters. It's the recording and review
of events within the Contextual Radar framework over time that can
then be mined for patterns.

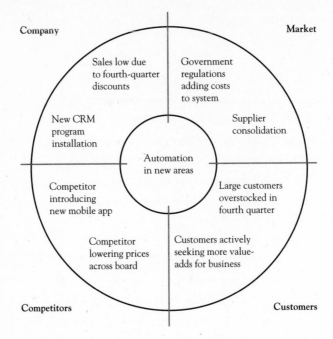

Figure 1.1   Contextual Radar—Q1

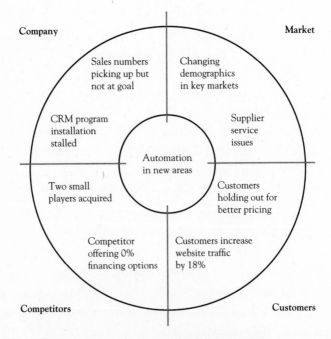

Figure 1.2   Contextual Radar—Q2

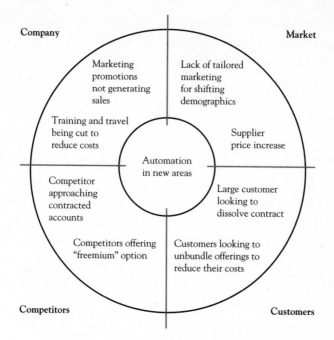

Figure 1.3 Contextual Radar—Q3

Table 1.1 Pattern Detector

Company	Market
Fourth-quarter discounts affecting sales throughout the year and conditioning customers to hold orders until that time.	Supplier consolidation reducing our profits.

Competitors	Customers
Competitor positioning at low end of the market through offerings, financing, and automation.	Competitors' activities causing customers to aggressively seek greater levels of value.

After reviewing the series of Contextual Radars, we can then look for and record patterns using the Pattern Detector, as seen in Table 1.1.

The Pattern Detector provides a forum for transforming business insights over time into meaningful patterns. Once the patterns are detected and described, thoughtful conversation around their meaning, impact, and warrant of resource allocation can occur. Without a device such as the Pattern Detector, reactivity becomes the primary modus operandi.

Systems

A strategist's ability to see the big picture involves not only the elements of the picture, but also how those elements are connected and what functions they serve. When these elements have connections and a purpose, we can refer to their whole as a system. The root of the word *system* comes from the Greek *synhistanai*, meaning "to place together."[10] As the first core skill of the advanced strategic thinker is to coalesce, or bring together, it's fitting that the concept of a system helps us do just that.

A soccer team is an example of a system. The elements are the players, coach, referee, ball, and field. The connections are the rules of soccer, teamwork, and tactical plan. The purpose may be one or more of the following: win the match, build fitness, enjoy oneself, and earn a living. One of the ways we know a soccer team is a system is because if we take away elements, connections, or purpose, the system is fundamentally changed. Remove the players or ball (elements), rules (connections), or score (purpose), and you no longer have a soccer game. As rules of thumb, if you cannot identify the elements, connections, or the effects they have upon each other, then they most likely do not form a system.

As scientist Donella Meadows explains, "A system is a set of things—people, cells, molecules—interconnected in such a way that they produce their own pattern of behavior over time. It's an interconnected set of elements that is coherently organized in a way that achieves something."[11] This description further builds on the concept of patterns described earlier. As a system develops, it generates patterns of behavior due to the connections between elements in an organized fashion. That's one of the reasons it's important to look at your business strategy as a system, involving your employees, customers, suppliers, competitors, and shareholders. Changes in any one of these elements or their connection (relationship) to others can fundamentally alter the course of your business. Strategic planning sessions that don't fully take into account the market, customers, competitors, and the company itself yield half-baked strategic plans that will crack under the pressure of changes in the system.

Understanding the systems that comprise your business is an important part of developing long-term strategy. Sound systems can lead to success, as Chipotle CEO Steve Ells noted, "Chipotle succeeds not because of the burritos. It works because of our system: fresh, local, sustainable ingredients, cooked with classic methods in an open kitchen where the customer can see everything, and served in a pleasing environment."[12] And a lack of systems thinking can lead to competitive disadvantage as Nokia CEO Stephen Elop lamented, "Our competitors aren't taking our market share with devices; they are taking our market share with an entire ecosystem."[13]

A useful exercise is to map out the system of the business. An Activity System Map provides a visual means of understanding the key elements and connections involved in mapping out a business strategy. It provides an elevated view of the business by capturing the strategy and activities, and the relationships between the two, on a single page. Designing an Activity System Map first requires the individual to step back and view the business from the high ground to better understand the strategic composition. It then drills down to assemble a conceptual framework, identifying the interrelationships and competencies of the key facets of the business. Once completed, the Activity System Map provides a clear and concise picture of the business, which enables leaders to more effectively set direction and allocate resources.

The Activity System Map consists of the strategic themes of the organization represented by large spheres, and the individual activities or tactics represented by small spheres. Between three and five strategic themes are appropriate to cover the primary hubs of strategy for a business. In addition to identifying the individual strategic themes and tactics, the Activity System Map highlights the strength of the relationships between the strategy and tactics. A solid line between two spheres indicates direct support and a dotted line indicates indirect support. Incorporating other elements such as suppliers, customers, and employees can add another dimension to the exercise. Based on secondary research, Figure 1.4 is a hypothetical example of an Activity System Map for Apple.

In this example, it is surmised that Apple's three strategic themes represented by the large spheres are design, integration, and convenience. These are the areas that would hypothetically receive a disproportionate amount of investment in order to drive the differentiated value of their offerings. Key activities and tactics (represented by the smaller spheres) such as the design of their own microprocessor chips, the Genius Bar, and the expansive virtual stores competently support their strategic themes. Summarizing the value of looking at your business with a system's lens is Harvard Business School professor Michael Porter: "Competitive advantage grows out of the *entire system* of activities. The fit among activities substantially reduces cost or increases differentiation. Beyond that, the competitive value of individual activities—or the associated skills, competencies, or resources—cannot be decoupled from the system or the strategy."[14]

Platforms

In the search for competitive advantage, many leaders have become fatigued by the hamster-wheel race to continually create new product and service features that are all too soon copied by the competition. They envy companies like Apple that design platforms, seemingly leap-frogging the head-to-head features battle that takes its toll on so many managers. While platforms may appear to be the panacea you've been searching for all along, they aren't an option for everyone.

To begin with, a platform requires the ability to look outside of your organization and see the potential for connections with others, often referred to as *complementors*. A platform is a foundation comprised of a product, service, technology, or system on which other complementary offerings can be built. Platforms serve to connect providers and consumers in ways that stand-alone offerings cannot.

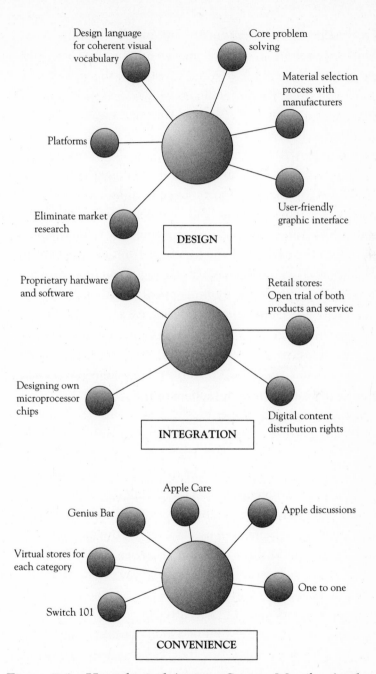

Figure 1.4   Hypothetical Activity System Map for Apple

To be considered a legitimate platform, the foundation is part of an evolving system and is not as valuable by itself. For instance, a video game console such as Xbox is considered a platform. It is part of an evolving system that includes gamers, software companies, and entertainment enterprises. Without the games or the players, it's not of much value by itself.

As far back as 2000, Apple founder Steve Jobs envisioned the Mac operating system as a digital hub for all of a user's content, including photos, video, music, and so on. The platform evolved into personal devices such as the iPod and iPad, and continues to transition as the digital hub moves to the cloud. Even a company not considered a pure technology firm, such as CVS, has used its retail outlets as platforms for a wide array of complementary offerings including basic healthcare (MinuteClinic), photography, and optical solutions.

The challenge facing platform providers is that they must engage both customers and the complementary offering developers in order for the platform to succeed. Returning to our example of the Xbox platform, on the one hand, if software game developers see gamers migrating to playing on their mobile devices, they may be less inclined to invest in developing games for the Xbox. With fewer quality games available for a device such as the Xbox, gamers would be further motivated to play on alternative devices such as phones or tablets, and a downward cycle would ensue. On the other hand, if gamers see the highest-quality, most engaging games being developed for the Xbox and not other platforms, then their loyalty to the Xbox platform would strengthen. As the number of users increases, the motivation for game developers to build for the platform also rises. These network effects, along with the high switching costs for gamers to move from one system to the next, act as a strategy shield for the platform provider.

A social network such as LinkedIn can also be described as a platform. First, it's part of an evolving system of workers moving from one job position or company to another. Second, without the numerous complementary offerings through partners such as Twitter, SlideShare, WordPress, and others, the value of LinkedIn would be greatly diminished. As LinkedIn co-founder Reid Hoffman said, "Social network platforms do best when they tap into one of the seven deadly sins. Facebook is ego. Zynga is sloth. LinkedIn is greed. With LinkedIn it's taking control of your economic destiny and improving how you operate as a professional and how you can develop a competitive advantage."[15]

Too often, a lack of differentiation in a company's core products or services is ignored or stubbornly dismissed until the firm becomes engulfed in full-fledged commoditization. Then the predictable product-line extension bandages are hastily stuck on the business, but do little to stem the flow of red ink. Research by professors Kim and Mauborgne found that 86 percent of business launches by companies were line extensions, but they generated only 39 percent of total profits. A mere 14 percent of launches consisted of newly differentiated offerings, yet these yielded a whopping 61 percent of total profits.[16] In a recent three-year study on innovation, only 13 percent of the world's leading consumer product companies were able to develop a breakthrough innovation. The authors of the study concluded, "The only thing keeping most big companies from creating new categories is their lack of imagination—their inability to see beyond what they're selling today."[17]

A rich source of platform innovation can come from the mental agility of leaders to move out of their strict mindset of providing either a product or a service, and instead look at the other category as an opportunity to develop their own complementors before outsiders do. Manufacturers exploring service complementors (Apple and their retail stores) or service providers exploring product complementors (Amazon.com and the Kindle) can reignite a company's growth.[18] In the automobile industry, increased cost/pricing transparency and hungry competitors have whittled away at profits. A number of auto manufacturers have worked to build on their platforms with services such as financing, insurance, warranties, maintenance, repair, Wi-Fi, navigation, and satellite radio. Their ability to enhance the service experience of an automobile may hold the key to growing profits in the long run.[19] Table 1.2 provides examples of platform complementors for different businesses.

Table 1.2   Platform Chain

Company	Customer	Need	Primary Offerings	Next-Layer Needs	Complementors
Apple	Baby boomers	Mobile computing	iPad, Mac	Personalized instruction	Own retail store
Amazon	Business travelers	Business knowledge	Online store	Convenient format	Kindle reader
Taco Bell	Teenagers	Hunger	Tacos	Unique taste	Doritos-flavored shells
LinkedIn	Job seekers	Optimal employment	Professional networks	Knowledge enhancement	Business content

How does one determine if their business is or could be platform-based? The following Platform Chain exercise can begin to clarify if your business is a candidate for platform development:

1. Identify your key customer segments.
2. Determine the main need currently fulfilled for these customers.
3. Record the primary offerings (products, services) that meet this need.
4. Uncover the next-layer needs this customer group has within this area.
5. Create solutions to satisfy these additional needs (complementors). Litmus test: without these complementors, the product/ service is of lesser value.

Establishing connections between the columns demonstrates there's opportunity to leverage a platform. If no platform currently exists, in what ways can the Platform Chain be modified to create one? If you're

Table 1.3 Platform Chain: Netflix Example

Customer	Need	Primary Offerings	Next-Layer Needs	Potential Complementors
20- to 30-year-old males	Convenient entertainment	DVDs, streaming	Variety and binge-viewing	Original content delivered in its entirety

a manufacturer, what services could be complementary to your products? If you're a service provider, what products could be complementary to your services?

Table 1.3 shows the Platform Chain being applied for Netflix.

Business Model

The holy grail of strategic thinking is, how do you come up with a business model that differentiates you and that creates value for your customers and by doing that, puts you in a unique position in your industry?
— Sam Palmisano, former chairman and CEO, IBM

At the foundation of a company is the business model. A business model is a structural description of how the organization creates, delivers, and captures value.[20] While the business model receives the white-hot spotlight of attention during a company's start-up phase, it is generally ignored and overlooked once the organization is launched. Attention then turns to sales and budgets, with little ongoing regard for the company's foundational construct. However, those companies that continue to develop and innovate their business models have shown to outperform industry peers by nearly 7 percent in total return to shareholders over a three-year period.[21] As *Fortune* magazine editor Geoff Colvin wrote, "Business-model innovation is the new essential competency. It's hard. It will separate tomorrow's winners from the losers."[22]

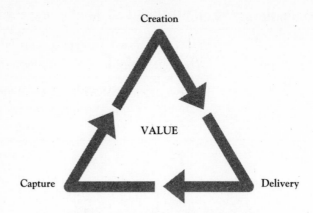

Figure 1.5   Business Model

If a company is functioning reasonably well, then it has a business model. The question becomes: How optimized is the business model for peak performance? Dysfunctional companies can often trace the cause of their troubles to cracks in the business model. As the definition of the business model centers on the creation, delivery, and capture of value, it is critical that these principal elements are fully explored and understood by leaders. (See Figure 1.5.)

Phase I of the Business Model: Value Creation

At the foundation of an organization's ability to create value are core competencies and capabilities. The terms *core competencies* and *capabilities* are often used interchangeably, which is both confusing and incorrect. A core competency is defined as a primary area of expertise. Popularized by authors Gary Hamel and C. K. Prahalad, a core competency represents the collective learning of an organization that brings together knowledge, skills, and technology, resulting in the ability to execute a value-producing process at a world-class level.[23] Simply put, a core competency is *what you know*. Common examples of core competencies include Honda's engine design and development, McDonald's food delivery system, and Canon's optics and imaging expertise. Keep in mind that a core competency isn't just something that you know pretty well; it's competitively important knowledge embedded in an organization that results in the ability to develop and execute to a world-class standard. To determine your company's core competencies, dig into the following three questions.

1. What are the areas of knowledge and skills your group possesses?
2. Are any of these areas currently best in industry?
3. Which of these areas produce the greatest differentiated value for customers?

Once the core competency or competencies have been identified, the capabilities can be established to deliver the value identified in the value proposition created in phase I of the business model. A capability is an organization's potential for using its resources to carry out specific activities to create value. Capabilities refer to the competitively relevant activities performed with key resources. They are the purposeful configuration of resources through activities designed to drive your strategy's success. Simply put, capabilities are *what you do*.

Common examples of capabilities include Walmart point-of-sales data analytics, eBay's alignment between software developers and marketers, and General Mills's brand management. When attempting to identify capabilities, it's easy to fall into the trap of recording a laundry list of things you do. Keep in mind that capabilities are the competitively relevant activities—the ones that use resources in a way that creates differentiated value for internal or external customers. To determine your organization's capabilities, start by asking the following three questions.

1. What are your group's top three capabilities?
2. What evidence supports these as being comprised of competitively relevant resources and activities?
3. What are the top three capabilities of your most dangerous competitor?

Once the core competencies and capabilities are identified, they can be used in the service of customers as articulated in the value proposition. The value proposition describes the rationale behind why customers would choose this particular offering over others. While the value proposition would appear to be an obvious given for the leaders of any organization, the research shows it's not. As authors Kaplan and Norton write, "In our research, we have found that although a clear definition of the value proposition is the single most important step in developing a strategy, approximately three-quarters of executive teams do not have consensus about this basic information."[24]

The value proposition can be broken down into four pieces:

1. Who: Customer to be served
2. What: Need to be met or job to be done
3. How: Approach to satisfy need or fulfill job
4. Benefit: Customer's advantage of using the offering

The value proposition begins with a specific customer segment and their unmet need—the job to be done. Authors Johnson, Christensen, and Kagermann have identified four barriers that prevent people from getting jobs completed: insufficient wealth, access, skill, and time.[25] Starting with these barriers for jobs to be done can immediately open up the range of possible solutions that can fulfill an unmet need. This job/need mindset also factors in non-traditional competitors or substitutes—solutions that are different but can fulfill the same function. For instance, beginning with a job to be done like cleaning a floor can provide innovative options ranging from the Dyson vacuum to a Swiffer to the Roomba cleaning robot. The value proposition for a Dyson vacuum might look like this:

Dyson serves middle-class and affluent customers with highly effective dirt removal from carpeted or non-carpeted floors by using bagless vacuum cleaners with cyclone technology in a stylish, see-through design, resulting in less time needed to clean.

In this example, we see the elements of the value proposition clearly identified using the following framework:

<u>*Dyson*</u> *serves* <u>*middle-class and affluent customers*</u> *with* <u>*highly*</u>
Company   **Who**

<u>*effective dirt removal*</u> *from carpeted or non-carpeted floors* <u>*by*</u>
  What

<u>*using bag-less vacuum cleaners with cyclone technology*</u> *in* <u>*a*</u>
                              How

<u>*stylish, see-through design*</u> *resulting in* <u>*less time needed to clean*</u>.
                              Benefit

In developing the elements of the value proposition for your offering, consider the following criteria:

1. **Customer:** The adage, "You can't be all things to all people"
   applies here. All potential customers are not your target customers. Your target customer is the group that finds the most
   value in your offering and provides you with the best economic
   return. Amazon.com CEO Jeff Bezos describes the importance
   of focusing on the customer, "We innovate by starting with the
   customer and working backwards. That becomes the touchstone
   for how we invent."[26] Strategist Keniche Ohmae echoes Bezos'
   sentiments when he writes, "Before you test yourself against the
   competition, your strategy takes shape in the determination to
   create value for customers."[27]

2. **Need/Job:** Giving careful consideration to the customer's unmet
   need or the job to be done forces you to shed the internally
   focused product/service mentality and concentrate on providing new or unique value. Using a customer's needs as the driver
   for evolving your offering challenges the status-quo approach
   that lulls so many leaders into complacency. As former Harvard
   Business School professor Theodore Levitt writes, "Customers
   attach value to a product in proportion to its perceived ability
   to help solve their problems or meet their needs."[28]

3. **Approach:** The approach signals to customers how your offering will provide value that other potential choices will not. It captures the method for delivering differentiated value that moves your offering to a unique position in the market. In short, the approach is your strategic direction, since it shows how you will allocate your resources to provide differentiated value to customers. Dyson offers his perspective on approach, "The root principle was to do things your way. It didn't matter how other people did it. And so I have sought out originality for its own sake, and modified it into a philosophy which demands difference from what exists even if only to redefine a stale market."[29]

4. **Benefit:** While it may seem obvious, it's important to include the benefit of using the offering. What is the resulting customer advantage of using your offering versus other offerings for the need/job at hand? Benefits generally fall into three categories: quality (more effective); convenience (saves time); and cost (saves money). A leader needs to be able to clearly articulate which of these benefits the offering provides and quantify it if possible in terms of efficacy, time, or money. As Washington University professor Todd Zenger writes, "Essentially, a leader's most vexing strategic challenge is not how to obtain or sustain competitive advantage—which has been the field of strategy's primary focus—but, rather, how to keep finding new, unexpected ways to create value."[30]

Phase II of the Business Model: Value Delivery

At its core, a business is a value delivery system. Once you've decided how to create value as described in the value proposition, you must then determine how to go about delivering that value. The deliver phase of the business model begins with the value chain, a useful tool in visualizing how an organization delivers value to its customers. While the value proposition takes an external view of value from the customer's perspective, the value chain takes the internal organizational view. It graphically describes the business unit or group's configuration of capabilities (resources and activities) to design, produce, market, sell, and service offerings for customers. Introduced by Harvard Business School professor Michael Porter in his book *Competitive Advantage*, he writes, "The value chain disaggregates a firm into its strategically relevant activities in order to understand the behavior of costs and the existing and potential sources of differentiation. A firm gains competitive advantage by performing these strategically important activities more cheaply or better than its competitors."[31]

Once the core competencies, capabilities, and value proposition have been crystallized, the value chain can be created to show how they will be employed in delivering value to customers. The value chain describes *how you do it*. It visually shows the sequence of activities that transform inputs such as raw materials and resources into the outputs that comprise the offerings to customers. The disaggregation of value by activity also serves to shine light on the areas most responsible for contributing to the differentiated value of the offering. In markets where competitors have similar capabilities, advantage can sometimes be had by altering the configuration of activities in the value chain. While competitors can more readily copy surface elements of your business including features and attributes, it is much more challenging for them to mimic all of your activities in their specified order that deliver value to customers.

Figure 1.6 provides a general value chain for the executive education industry. The five primary value-chain activities are creation, design, marketing, delivery, and support. Three examples are provided to highlight the different approaches to providing executives with business education. The examples demonstrate the various ways to configure activities in order to provide a certain type of value to a particular customer segment. The offerings range from customized content delivered in-person to intact teams to more general content delivered virtually to individuals.

The different approaches will appeal to different customers based on their specific needs and budget. One approach is not inherently better than the others. They each offer a different mix of value. Some executives may prefer learning content with their intact team at their

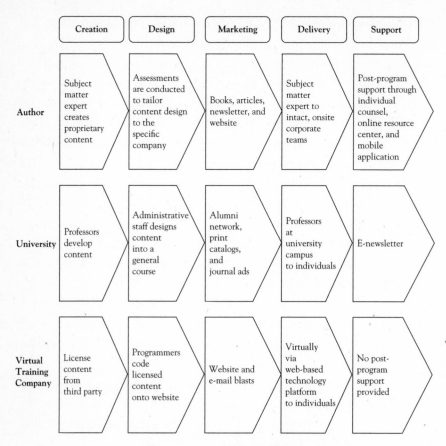

Figure 1.6 Value Chain

company headquarters to speed up the practical application of knowledge and skills to their current business issues. Other executives might prefer working alongside managers from other industries to stimulate new thinking while enjoying the prestige of a highly recognized business school. Still others may prefer learning online at their own pace for a fraction of the cost of the other two options. Working through the value-chain exercise for your business will ensure that the chosen approach is optimal based on your core competency and capabilities relative to the needs of the target market.

The final aspect of the delivery phase of a business model is the channel. The channel is the access point for customers to obtain your offerings. It represents the conduit between your offering and the user. The channel is *where you offer it*. Effective channel selection means customers have the opportunity to see and purchase your offerings. Poor channel selection may mean potential customers never see— and therefore never purchase—your offerings. There's a rich history of superior products and services that disappeared into the Bermuda Triangle of business because of the inability to manage the channel.

One such example is the Michelin PAX System. Unlike traditional tires, which become useless in the event of a puncture, the revolutionary PAX run-flat tire can be driven flat for 125 miles at speeds of 55 mph. When Michelin began developing the tire in 1992, it believed that this innovation would be as big a win as the introduction of the radial tire 50 years earlier. The company spent years and untold riches developing the tire, which it trademarked under the PAX label.

However, when the tire was finally introduced in 1997, consumers couldn't buy it. The tires connect to a vehicle's electronic system, so they could be used only in vehicles designed to accommodate them. Since electronics are added in when new cars are designed, Michelin had to wait until a willing manufacturer's design window opened. At the time, an average auto manufacturer took three to four years to move a car from design to volume production. So, even if the tire was fortunate enough to be designed into a car model that enjoys market success, Michelin's best case was that volume sales would begin three to four years after the tire was introduced. As it happened, even the few willing auto manufacturers with whom Michelin coordinated design cycles initially offered it as an option on only a very limited set of models.

Michelin needed to consider other intermediaries in the channel configuration as well, all of whom needed to buy into the concept before end customers could weigh in with their purchase decisions. Specifically, repair shops would need to invest in new equipment and training, and dealers would need to understand and support the PAX system. More than a decade after its introduction, Michelin's PAX system tires were standard equipment on only a handful of car models sold in the mid-2000s.

Although the run-flat tire hasn't taken off in the commercial channel, it did meet with success in the defense market, where it is used as a substitute for track treads in vehicles such as the U.S. Army's Stryker troop carrier. With fewer intermediaries, more concentrated buyers, and greater perceived benefit, the military channel was a better fit, at least in the short run. The example serves as a reminder that failure in one channel is not necessarily a death knell, but can also be a wake-up call.

The potential channels for your offerings include both direct (e.g., internet, sales force, retail outlet) and indirect (e.g., manufacturer's representatives, wholesalers, outside retail stores) options. Determining the appropriate channel mix should take into account the current level of customer awareness for the offerings, internal capabilities, volume sales goals, requisite profit margins, and the threshold level of support and service desired. Use these three questions to get started:

1. What are the pros and cons of direct versus indirect channels for your offerings?
2. Which channels provide you with the greatest combination of access to target customers and profit margin?
3. How can your core competencies and capabilities be used to optimize these channels?

Phase III of the Business Model: Value Capture

The litmus test of a sound business model is its ability to deliver customer value profitably. The third phase of the business model asks how you will capture the value generated by your offerings. A good idea unsupported by a financial formula for success remains nothing more than a good idea. The capture phase requires a firm understanding of the economic underpinnings of the offerings provided to customers to ensure sufficient cash flow and profit will fuel the business into the future.

There are four ingredients to consider when establishing how you will capture the value generated from your offering:

1. Price: The amount customers pay for the offering
2. Revenue: Price multiplied by volume sold
3. Cost: Expenditure of resources to provide offering
4. Profit: Revenue minus cost.

These four elements can be calculated for older offerings in mature markets as well as new offerings in emerging markets. The price can be identified in both quantitative and relative terms. A number alone, say $100, is insufficient for understanding how that price will position our offering versus the competition. Does the $100 price point represent a premium position in the market, a moderate position, or a discount relative to competitors? Therefore, it's helpful to identify price in both quantitative (e.g., $100) and relative (e.g., premium) terms.

When it comes to revenue, price is multiplied by the expected volume (e.g., number of customers, units per customer per transaction, transactions per customer) to determine the amount of money to be made from the offering. While an *asset sale*, such as a bicycle purchase, may be the most common form of revenue, there are now many additional ways to generate revenue.[32] The following are examples of how major corporations generate revenue:

- Bill Gates built Microsoft's software fortune through *licensing*.
- Enterprise Rent-A-Car became an industry giant by *renting* cars primarily in community settings.
- The *Wall Street Journal* has continued to produce revenue through both print and online *subscriptions*.
- FedEx has garnered a large share of shipping revenues through *usage fees* for the delivery of packages from point A to point B.
- Google has used *advertising* as a primary revenue stream at the foundation of their business.
- Financial investment firms like Charles Schwab have built vast sums of wealth by connecting investors with financial products through intermediary services charging *brokerage fees*.

With a variety of options at a leader's disposal, a company's success can be greatly enhanced or stymied by their choice of revenue stream.

It seems that the first place leaders turn to when a business model isn't working is to the cost component. Costs are described in many different ways, including fixed, variable, direct, indirect, and sunk, depending on the structure in place. While cutting costs is a common reflexive response when a business is not generating sufficient profit, it may only provide short-term relief at the expense of long-term growth. The key is a solid understanding of the costs involved in providing the offering and how they contribute to the value being produced.

In the previous discussion of the value chain, once the activities have been identified and arranged in order of use, costs can be assigned to each. This exercise helps to establish a clear view of both the benefit and the cost of each activity in the value chain so a leader can ensure any cost reductions are not jeopardizing the important value-generating activities. For a professional services firm providing accounting software solutions, cutting costs in research and development activities may lead to short-term profit but a long-term loss of valuable intellectual property. However, an industrial supplier of construction materials able to reduce costs in their manufacturing processes can boost margins, and potentially pass along some of the cost savings to customers in the form of lower prices.

The final element of the capture phase is profit. Research by UCLA business professor Richard Rumelt showed that the number-one factor in a business unit's profitability was its choice of strategy.[33] While we've covered price, revenue, and costs—the components of profit—it's still important to isolate and study profit. As professor Paul Rubin writes:

> *Profit maximization is good because it leads directly to maximum benefits for consumers. Profits provide the incentive for firms to do what consumers want. . . . What if a business does not maximize profits? Then it is either not making the products that consumers want the most, or it is not producing its products at the lowest cost. In either case, consumers are harmed.*[34]

A long list of companies have been lured into the rocks of bankruptcy by the siren song of growth for growth's sake. In fact, growth at the expense of profit can lead to a colossal collapse. A five-year study of 600 companies showed that less than half the companies with annual revenue growth rates of 5 percent or more also attained increasing operating margins. In fact, more than 20 percent experienced an absolute decline in profits. As the researchers concluded, "While revenue growth must be part of any strategy to enhance profitability and shareholder value, it's not sufficient in itself."[35]

When it comes to generating profit, you have two primary levers: revenue and costs. You can increase revenue through greater volume, higher prices, or lower costs. Which lever you pull will be determined by a number of factors including the context of the business, competitive landscape, core competencies, and capabilities to name just a few. But recent research by Michael Raynor and Mumtaz Ahmed on business performance shows the revenue lever may be more effective than the cost lever. They concluded:

> . . . by an overwhelming margin, exceptional companies generate superior profits through higher revenue than their rivals, with higher prices more popular than higher volume . . . the highest-performing companies tended to rely more on higher gross margins than on lower cost as a source of performance advantage, suggesting a better before cheaper bias.[36]

To summarize, the three phases of a business model can be described as follows:

Phase I: Value Creation

Core competency: Primary area of expertise (what you know)

Capabilities: Activities performed with key resources (what you do)

Value proposition: Rationale for the offering (customer, need/job, approach, benefit)

Phase II: Value Delivery

Value chain: Configuration of capabilities to provide value (how you do it)

Channels: Customer access points for offerings (where you offer it)

Phase III: Value Capture

Price: Amount customers pay for the offering

Revenue: Price multiplied by volume sold

Cost: Expenditure of resources to provide offering

Profit: Revenues minus costs

Profitable Growth

The point of coalescing insights into strategic direction is to generate profitable growth. Ford Motor Company President and CEO Alan Mulally realized that was his charge when he took over the leadership reigns at Ford in 2006 as it posted a $12.6 billion loss. Implementing his One Ford Plan, he has steadily driven the American auto manufacturer back into profitability. Mulally explains, "Business is about profitable growth and creating value. So everything, every input that you get, the filter that it goes through is, what's the plan to profitably grow the business?"[37] Starbuck's CEO Howard Schultz echoes this approach when he says, "When you look at growth as a strategy, it becomes somewhat seductive, addictive. But growth should not be—and is not—a strategy . . . as we return the company to growth, it'll be disciplined, profitable growth for the right reasons—a different kind of growth."[38]

Building pipelines of continuous, profitable growth is the lifeblood of any business. Therefore, it's important to understand the potential levers for growth as well as the pitfalls that can stall it. Research was conducted on 500 companies to better understand what causes successful organizations to stop growing and struggle financially for extended periods of time. The study found that 87 percent of stall points, a term for the start of a prolonged financial decline, are caused by factors that are within management's control. A staggering 70 percent of these stall factors result from choices about strategy. The effects of these stall points can be devastating. The researchers reported that, "On average, companies lose 74 percent of their market capitalization as measured against the S&P 500 index in the decade surrounding a growth stall."[39]

As the results show, your ability to craft, communicate, and execute sound strategy will determine the firm's financial results. It's one thing to ask a manager to reduce costs by 15 percent. She will readily come up with a laundry list of ways to reduce costs. It's an entirely different thing to ask a manager to profitably grow the business 15 percent. She will most likely be stumped or trot out the same old line-up of tired tactics. When senior leaders are tasked with growing a business, many quickly turn to the acquisition of other companies. Mergers and acquisitions capture many of the headlines in business publications, but do they capture profitable growth? While some companies have become experts at identifying M&A candidates and then successfully blending the new business into the existing one, it's not necessarily the norm. Multiple studies over the past 20 years have shown that the majority of acquisitions actually destroy their own shareholder's value.[40]

To spur your thinking on organic growth, it's helpful to have an understanding of the range of potential pathways to increase profits. A tool I've developed to help leaders explore their growth options is the Strategy Spectrum. The Strategy Spectrum visually lays out the full gamut of levers for creating new value for customers that can stimulate profitable growth. There are six levers that comprise the Strategy Spectrum:

1. **What:** Offerings (products/services)
2. **Who:** Potential target customers
3. **Why:** Customer need or job fulfilled
4. **Where:** Channels to access offerings
5. **When:** Time of access to offerings
6. **How:** Activities

Beginning with the current business model, items are placed into each column representing the business as it operates today. Then new items borrowed from other companies and industries are used to complete the columns. The key is to play with combinations from the various columns to generate new ways to profitably grow the business. Table 1.4 is an example of the Strategy Spectrum as it might be applied by a financial services firm.

Playing with the elements from the different columns, one combination would be to provide financial education to teenagers at high schools during lunch to educate them on finances using a mobile app. Another example might have the firm offer debt reduction to trade laborers using mobile units at job sites to provide financial relief via videos.

The Strategy Spectrum offers a graphical way to explore the range of options available in stimulating profitable growth for a business. As you develop the Strategy Spectrum, it's helpful to pull in people from various functional areas and outside the company to offer different frames of reference and a greater variety of menu items. If your company primarily provides products or hard goods, consider what types of complementary services could help them more effectively or efficiently complete their jobs to be done (e.g., truck manufacturer offering maintenance and logistics services). In the same token, if your company is a service provider, think about the services your customers need with the products to fulfill their needs (e.g., internet search engine selling mobile phones) and populate the Strategy Spectrum with those ideas as well.

Another tool for exploring new ways to profitably grow is the Value Mining Matrix. The Value Mining Matrix considers customers and the jobs they need fulfilled. As you'll recall, these are two of the primary elements of the value proposition discussed earlier. In this exercise, customers and jobs are used to catalyze thinking on methods for creating new value. Customers are thought of as current, those you're actively marketing to, selling to, serving, or supporting today. Or, customers are thought of as potential, meaning groups or types of customers you're not actively marketing to, selling to, serving or supporting

Table 1.4 Strategy Spectrum

What	Who	Where	When	Why	How
Investment	Business people	Colleges	At night	Education	Kiosk
Insurance	Teens	Airport	Weekends	Advice	Offices
Estate planning	Trade laborers	Retirement communities	Graduations	Financial relief	Mobile app
Financial education	Retirees	High school	Lunch	Wealth creation	Videos
Debt reduction	Kids	Mobile units	At work	Business growth	One-to-one meeting
Real estate	Travelers	Mega churches	During school	Investment opportunity	Group seminars
Business planning	College students	Big box stores	While traveling	Security	TV

today. These potential customers may be influencers, decision makers, or end users that may find value in what you're able to provide.

The job axis views customer jobs that need to be fulfilled as either existing today (current needs) or emerging. Emerging jobs would consist of future needs that customers would find value in having fulfilled by your organization. The jobs to be done may not be identified, talked about or even noticed by your customers, but often manifest themselves as the problems, pains, or challenges they face. While "Voice of the Customer" programs are helpful in gaining a deeper understanding of their reactions to current offerings, they may not elicit the deeper insights about their real needs. These deeper insights can often be gleaned by simply observing your customers in their day-to-day activities and noting the issues, problems, and challenges that arise. Creating a list of their "jobs to be done" is an effective way to begin the Value Mining process. Figure 1.7 is the Value Mining Matrix with an example in each quadrant.

Starting in the lower-left quadrant, an example of a company finding new profitable growth by fulfilling an existing need for current customers is CVS Caremark's MinuteClinic. Their current customer

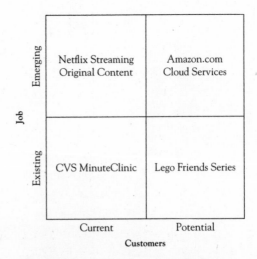

Figure 1.7   Value Mining Matrix

base had a need for an existing service, which was quick, convenient care for non-emergency medical conditions. This job was not being fulfilled adequately by physicians, who require appointments that are often not convenient or soon enough for patients. By offering the MinuteClinics in their store locations, CVS Caremark was able to drive profitable growth by serving current customers with an existing job to be done (quick, convenient medical care).

In the lower-right quadrant, new profitable growth comes from potential customers with an existing need to be filled. The example here is from Lego, the manufacturer of plastic bricks in sets of branded series. Lego was able to tap into the existing need for an entertaining toy that helps to promote children's spatial skills. The company chose to focus on young girls, who had been less engaged with the brand than boys. The Lego Friends series provides young girls with the opportunity to build, socialize, and create with female characters in settings such as horse stables and campgrounds.

In the upper-left quadrant, Netflix provide an example of a company generating growth by serving current customers with an emerging need that was previously unfilled. The need was to find new television programs that can be consumed in a binge format instead of waiting a week to watch the next episode. The convenience of being able to stream the original content on different devices provides current customers of Netflix with both new content and new access to entertainment.

Finally, in the upper-right quadrant, Amazon.com's cloud services has tapped into potential customers with the emerging unfulfilled need of hosting content in a conveniently accessed medium. By providing on-demand computer services via the cloud to other businesses ranging from Netflix to NASA, Amazon.com has generated profitable growth by helping new customers get a job done.

Too often, ideas for growth are seen from a product point-of-view, instead of a need or job to be fulfilled perspective. The Value Mining Matrix shifts your focus to both current and potential customers and existing and emerging jobs to be done can offer new avenues for profitable growth. As ideas fill the four quadrants, it will become apparent that they may require different time frames to bring to market. Once you've generated the ideas, you can begin to place them into one of three time horizons.[41] Horizon 1 consists of ideas to grow the business during the next year as you extend and defend your current business. Horizon 2 is comprised of ideas to generate profitable growth in the next two to three years by changing an element or elements of your business model. Horizon 3 includes ideas for growth beyond three years that may require new capabilities or a new business model to carry the organization into the future.

Growth Horizons

Horizon 1: First year; extend and defend current business.

Horizon 2: Years two and three; modify parts of the business model.

Horizon 3: After three years; consider new business model.

Strategy and Innovation

Strategy and innovation are often shown to be two primary contributors to sustained financial excellence and competitive advantage. The common denominator for both strategy and innovation is insight. An insight is described as the joining together of two or more pieces of information or data in a unique way to come up with a new approach, new product, new service, or new solution that delivers value. Insights come from the ability to wade through the waves of input we receive each day and mentally connect the dots in new and creative ways. As Apple founder Steve Jobs remarked, "Creativity is just connecting things."[42]

Prolific inventor James Dyson built his billion-dollar business through insights on what frustrated people. His first significant invention—the Ballbarrow—was a wheelbarrow that used a ball instead of a wheel. This insight came from the frustration people had with the wheels getting stuck in the mud and rendered useless. Dyson recounted how insight also fueled the birth of his famous vacuum:

Sometimes you see a bit of technology working in one application and you wonder whether that might solve the problem that's been gnawing at your brain. That's how the vacuum cleaner worked. I went to a lumberyard one day to buy some tinder and saw these massive 30-foot high cyclones collecting the sawdust on top of the roof. So I rushed home and started building small cyclones.[43]

Innovation, defined most simply as creating new value for customers, begins with an insight. The insight often centers on a solution to a problem or way to fulfill an unmet need of a customer. To create new value, you need this insight. Business strategy is defined as the intelligent allocation of limited resources through a unique system of activity to outperform the competition in serving customers. The only way to truly intelligently allocate resources is to have strong insight into how your product or service provides value to customers in ways that are different than competitive offerings. Doing the same things in the same way as the competition is a common formula for bankruptcy.

If the value is new, then it's likely to be different from current offerings. As James Dyson said when he seized leadership of the upright vacuum market from Hoover with his cyclone technology, "And so I have sought originality for its own sake, and modified it into a philosophy which demands difference from what exists if only to redefine a stale market."[44] The intent then of both business strategy and innovation is to create value for customers. Too often, in the day-to-day competitive battles and the weeds of the business, we lose sight of the fact that competitive advantage is nothing more than "creating superior value for customers." Innovation is the continual hunt for new value; strategy is ensuring that we configure our resources in the best way possible to deliver that value.

Types of Innovation

The goal of creating new value is something that many managers aspire to and few truly achieve. Prior to attempting to create new value, it's wise to understand how the new value will enhance the position of your business. When a leader embarks on innovation efforts, there are four potential outcomes:

1. Differentiation: providing a distinct offering that leads to new profits

2. Neutralization: eliminating a gap in offerings or performance relative to the competition and market standards

3. Productivity: increasing efficiency or efficacy of processes in order to reduce costs

4. Waste: efforts that don't result in the first three outcomes and miss the mark of providing new value at an acceptable cost[45]

Obviously, no one is seeking waste, the fourth potential outcome of innovation efforts. The key to avoiding wasted innovation efforts is to understand the strategic context the business is in and select the type of innovation initiatives that have the greatest likelihood of economic value at that point in the category's evolution. As Harvard Business School Dean Nitin Nohria wrote, "A lack of contextual sensitivity can trip up even the most brilliant of executives . . . the risks of contextual insensitivity are concrete. If you can't read the business landscape, you risk leading your organization in the wrong direction."[46]

As you identify and vet ideas for creating new value, research by author Geoffrey Moore provides a powerful analytical framework for matching different types of innovation options with the context of the business.[47] Building off the value disciplines research of Michael Treacy and Fred Wiersema, Moore proposes that there are 14 different types of innovation that could be leveraged when aligned with the appropriate category life cycle (growth, mature, or declining).[48] The value-disciplines concept uses research to support the fact that financially successful firms focus a disproportionate amount of resources in one of the following three value disciplines:

1. **Product leadership:** cutting edge offerings

2. **Customer intimacy:** tailored solutions

3. **Operational excellence:** low cost and/or convenience

Coupled with these concepts are the four phases of the buying hierarchy described by professor Clayton Christensen:[49]

Functionality ➡ Convenience ➡ Reliability ➡ Price

The buying hierarchy explains that when no current offering satisfies a customer's need for functionality, the decision-making factor becomes functionality. Once two or more offerings demonstrate adequate functionality, the buying criterion shifts to reliability—does the offering consistently perform at the desired level? As reliability is shown by two or more players, the purchase decision moves to convenience—is it easy to use and hassle-free? Finally, if offerings demonstrate reliable functionality and similar convenience, the decision point in the buying hierarchy shifts to price.

The buying hierarchy can be overlaid onto the Innovation Zones framework from left to right, with functionality lining up with product leadership, reliability and convenience with customer intimacy, and price with operational excellence. As an example, working on customer intimacy innovation initiatives for an offering in a relatively new market will probably not be as productive because customers will be more focused on functionality (*Does it work?*) and reliability (*Does it work consistently?*).

Figure 1.8 shows the stages of the category life cycle aligned with the value disciplines and 14 types of innovation. According to Moore, in a growth market, the product leadership value discipline tends to produce more effective types of innovation that relate to disruption, product, application, and platform. Here, the market is searching for improvements in functionality and reliability. In an early maturing market, the customer-intimacy value discipline has a greater likelihood of yielding fruitful innovation in the form of line extensions, enhancement, marketing, and user experience. At this point in the buying hierarchy, market entrants are reaching parity as it relates to an offering's features and benefits. Therefore, an investment in customer intimacy types of innovation helps deepen relationships with current customers.

As the category life cycle moves to late maturity, the operational excellence zone featuring value engineering, integration, process, and value migration innovation offer greater chances of producing value. While both in the mature market part of the category life cycle, the

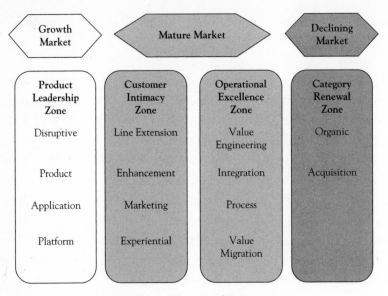

Figure 1.8   Types of Innovation

Customer Intimacy Zone works on differentiating the offering by making it more attractive to the customer (e.g., external, demand side). The Operational Excellence Zone focuses on enhancing the offering from the perspective of the company (e.g., internal, supply side). Finally, as the market declines, efforts around organic innovation and acquisitions provide opportunity for creating new value.

There are 14 different types of innovation that can create new value, depending on where you are in the category life cycle and what capabilities your firm possesses. Table 1.5 provides brief definitions and examples of the types of innovation in the Product Leadership Zone.

Table 1.6 provides brief definitions and examples of the types of innovation in the customer intimacy zone.

Table 1.7 provides brief definitions and examples of the types of innovation in the Operational Excellence Zone.

Finally, Table 1.8 provides brief definitions and examples of the types of innovation in the Category Renewal Zone.

The following questions can help you facilitate thinking and conversation around using the Innovation Zone framework to find areas for creating new value:

Which phase of the category lifecycle are we in: growth, early maturity, late maturity, or decline?

Which phase of the buying hierarchy are potential customers looking to satisfy: functionality, reliability, convenience, or price?

Table 1.5 Product Leadership Zone

Type	Definition	Example
Disruptive	Discontinuous technology change or business model	CVS Caremark MinuteClinics
Application	Develop new markets for existing products by finding untapped uses for them	LinkedIn for talent management
Product	Differentiate via features and functions not currently available	Corning's Gorilla Glass for iPhones
Platform	Create a simplifying layer over a complex layer	Facebook

Table 1.6 Customer Intimacy Zone

Type	Definition	Example
Line extension	Structural changes to offering to create a unique subcategory	Lego Friends series for girls
Enhancement	Alter a single dimension of the offering to stimulate interest	Coors Light Cold Activation bottles
Marketing	Create a unique interaction with a prospective customer during the purchase process	Apple retail stores
Experiential	Experience of the offering as primary value driver	Xbox Live gaming with users around the world

Table 1.7   Operational Excellence Zone

Type	Definition	Example
Value engineering	Remove cost from materials and manufacturing of offering without altering benefits to customer	LCD televisions
Integration	Decrease customer's cost of maintaining a complex operation by offering a centrally managed system	Amazon.com cloud services
Process	Remove waste from the processes producing the offering	IKEA
Value migration	Alter business model elements to shift from commodity points to profit points in value chain	Netflix original content distributed through streaming video versus DVDs delivered by mail

Table 1.8   Category Renewal Zone

Type	Definition	Example
Organic	Employ resources to reposition into a growth phase	McDonald's specialty drinks
Acquisition	Merge or acquire	Google (Motorola)

Based on the phase of the category lifecycle and buying hierarchy you're in, utilize the following questions from the corresponding Innovation Zone to stimulate thinking:

Product Leadership Zone—Innovation Types

Disruptive: How can we develop offerings that are simpler, more convenient, and less expensive than established offerings to attract new or less demanding customers?

Application: How can we use our capabilities to develop new markets for our existing offerings and what untapped uses can they fill?

Product: What functions and features can we create in our offerings to fulfill customer's unmet needs and jobs to be done?

Platform: Is there an opportunity to create a simplifying layer over a complex layer in the market to provide value to customers?

Customer Intimacy Zone—Innovation Types

Line extension: How can we modify one or more dimensions of our current offering to create a new subcategory that expands the market by bringing in new customers?

Enhancement: What one dimension of our offering can we improve to increase share of wallet with existing customers?

Marketing: How can we make the current offering more competitive by leveraging other elements of the marketing mix (promotion, place, price)?

Experiential: Is there an opportunity to create differentiated value within the time span customers are engaged with our offering?

Operational Excellence Zone—Innovation Types

Value Engineering: In what ways can we comprehensively remove cost from our system and still provide the same level of benefits in our offering?

Integration: Is there a way to pull together different components of a business and provide customers with a single system?

Process: In what ways could we enhance or cost-reduce the process used to produce our offering?

Value migration: Which areas of the industry value chain could we move into that would provide greater profit points?

Category Renewal Zone—Innovation Types

Organic: In what ways could we use our capabilities to transition into a growth category?

Acquisition: What offerings could we acquire that would position us favorably for the future?

1,000-Foot View

A pattern is a combination of qualities, acts, or characteristics forming a consistent arrangement.

A system is a set of things—people, cells, molecules—interconnected in such a way that they produce their own pattern of behavior over time. It's an interconnected set of elements that is coherently organized in a way that achieves something.

An Activity System Map provides an elevated view of the business by capturing the strategy and tactics, and the relationships between the two, on a single page.

A platform is a foundation comprised of a product, service, technology, or system on which other complementary offerings can be built.

A business model is a structural description of how the organization creates, delivers, and captures value. The three phases of the business model and their components include:

Phase I: Value Creation

Core competency: Primary area of expertise (what you know)

Capabilities: Activities performed with key resources (what you do)

Value proposition: Rationale for the offering (customer, need/job, approach, benefit)

Phase II: Value Delivery

Value chain: Configuration of capabilities to provide value (how you do it)

Channels: Customer access points for offerings (where you offer it)

Phase III: Value Capture

Price: Amount customers pay for the offering

Revenue: Price multiplied by volume sold

Cost: Expenditure of resources to provide offering

Profit: Revenues minus costs

A Strategy Spectrum is comprised of six levers:

1. **What:** Offerings (products/services)
2. **Who:** Potential target customers
3. **Why:** Customer need or job fulfilled
4. **Where:** Channels to access offerings
5. **When:** Time of access to offerings
6. **How:** Activities

The Value Mining Matrix considers both customers and jobs to catalyze thinking on methods for creating new value.

Innovation is creating new value for customers.

There are 14 different types of innovation used strategically depending on the stage of market maturity the business is in.

Compete

To strive together to achieve a goal,
we may never know a more noble role.

The archetype of the Renaissance man, Leonardo da Vinci excelled at many disciplines including painting, sculpture, architecture, and engineering to name just a few. In 1483, he created one of the first and most famous designs for the precursor of today's helicopter, commonly referred to as the "aerial screw." Made from reed, linen, and wire, his invention was designed to compress air to obtain flight through the unique spiral shape of its sail. While da Vinci's model would not have been able to take flight due to weight constraints, he nevertheless provided inspiration for future designers.

It was during the Italian Renaissance that da Vinci and his counterparts fanned the flames of competition in the arts. They introduced the concept of *paragone*, which means that one art form—be it sculpture, painting, or design—was perceived as being superior to others. This concept evolved into monetary contests sponsored by wealthy patrons, where the artists themselves were in direct competition with one another. Far from hindering creativity, the act of one artist having to compete directly with another artist was encouraged. Da Vinci wrote:

You will be ashamed to be counted among draughtsmen if your work is inadequate, and this disgrace must motivate you to profitable study. Secondly a healthy envy will stimulate you to become one of those who are praised more than yourself, for the praises of others will spur you on.[1]

The word *compete* originates from the Latin *competere*, meaning "to strive together."[2] To compete means to strive toward a goal. In attempting to reach the goal, we strive with others seeking that same goal, which supplies the motivational catalyst for us to try harder. Back in 1921, Charles Schwab was the president of the United States Steel Company. In *How to Win Friends and Influence People*, Dale Carnegie recounts one of Schwab's noteworthy leadership moments during a visit to an underperforming steel mill. In steelmaking, each complete melting operation produces what is called a *heat*. As the day shift was about to head home, Schwab asked how many heats they had completed during their shift. The answer was six. In chalk, Schwab wrote a six in the middle of the factory floor. When the night shift arrived, they asked what the number meant, and they were told that it was the number of heats produced by the day shift—and that Schwab himself had written it. Not to be outdone, at the end of the night shift, the evening workers had completed seven heats, and changed the number on the floor to reflect their hard day's work. Naturally, the day shift came in and the game was on. Soon, the plant was one of the most productive in the company.

Whether it was thousands of years ago during the Ancient Olympic games in Greece, hundreds of years ago during the Italian Renaissance, or this past century in American business, competition has motivated individuals to higher levels of performance. In fact, research shows that in the arts, athletics, and academics, the act of competing helps most people perform at a higher level.[3] In their intriguing book *Top Dog*, authors Po Bronson and Ashley Merryman summarize their findings on competition when they write, "The real benefit of competition is not winning—it is improved performance. Competition liberates, or generates, hidden reserves of additional effort. Competitors discover an extra gear."[4]

This motivational aspect of competition is even stronger when people know that they are just slightly behind those they are competing with. An analysis of data from 60,000 basketball games, including 18,000 National Basketball Association (NBA) games, found teams that were losing by one point at halftime were more likely to win than teams that were ahead by one point at halftime.[5] Following a similar theme, professor Jonah Berger of the Wharton School of Business conducted research with people who believed they were competing to make the fastest keystrokes on a keyboard with someone in another room. Halfway through, the participants were given feedback indicating if they were ahead, even, slightly behind, or far behind. When the participants finished and the data was tabulated, professor Berger concluded, "The results were clear. Effort increased dramatically only for people who believed they were slightly behind in the competition."[6] Winning in any endeavor is often a result of competing to one's maximum potential. And as a leader, isn't that precisely what you're trying to help your people do: perform to their full potential?

Competitive Condition

A condition is a situation with respect to circumstances. The term condition can be applied to a number of different arenas, from medicine (what is the patient's condition?) to sports (what are the conditions of the golf course?). Before physicians prescribe treatment, they first want to understand their patients' conditions (e.g., symptoms, age, allergies, medical history, etc.). Before professional golfers select a club to hit a particular shot, they consult with their caddies on the conditions of the hole (e.g., wind speed, wind direction, slope of fairway, slope of green, etc.). Not accounting for a 20 mph headwind could cost a golfer the tournament title and hundreds of thousands of dollars.

How would you describe your business condition? While the responses may range from optimistic to hopeless, your condition could be described as leader, challenger, or spectator. A leader is a company, product, or service that has market leadership and is in the position of protecting the business they have while looking for new, profitable growth. A challenger actively seeks ways to increase brand awareness and expand business. A spectator is a "me-too" type that operates in either a constantly reactive or mind-numbingly passive way. The goals and strategies you set can be conditional, depending on which of these positions you find yourself in.

Leader

When a new challenger enters the leader's market, there exists the temptation to immediately react with a flurry of tactics or completely ignore the new player altogether. But, before either of these approaches should even be considered, a thoughtful assessment of the new entrant will provide a range of available options to strategically manage the situation. The following are the top 10 questions to catalyze your thought process and initiate a productive conversation around the topic of the new challenger:

1. Does the challenger's offering provide different benefits from our offering?
2. Do the challenger's unique benefits include functionality, quality, reliability, convenience, and/or cost?
3. Does the challenger enter the market with a different business model?
4. Does the challenger's business model differ from ours in how they create, deliver, or capture value?
5. What is the challenger's value proposition?
6. What is the challenger's core competency?
7. What are the challenger's top three capabilities?
8. Does the challenger's offering target the same customer segments as our offering?
9. Is the challenger capable of taking away our current customers?
10. Should we respond to the challenger at this time or just monitor their activity?

If the analysis justifies responding to the challenger's offering, there are typically four strategic approaches that can be taken. As a market leader, in addition to the offensive growth goal and strategies reviewed in the "Discipline #1: Coalesce" section, there are generally two additional goals: retain customers and slow the rate of customer defection. In determining their strategies, they will look to leverage their strengths and neutralize rivals. Figure 2.1 shows the options a leader has in developing strategies to protect their business, as first described by professor John Roberts.

	Utilize Strengths	Neutralize Competitors
Maintain Customers	*Critical Mass* Retain customers by focusing on your product's advantages and experience, including innovations	*Blunting* Retain customers by neutralizing the perceived benefits of challengers
Minimize Rate of Defection	*Status-Quo* Emphasize the positive current use of the product and the lost benefits that would result from switching to a competitor	*Deceleration* Decrease loss rate of customers by positioning competitor advantages as minimal

Figure 2.1   Leader Strategies

McDonald's is a good example of a leader able to retain its customers by leveraging the strengths of consistency and location, while continuing to expand into healthy menu items and beverages. Dunkin Donuts has also defended its market by blunting rivals' (e.g., Starbucks) perceived advantages, showing how ordinary folks prefer the taste of Dunkin Donuts coffee. In the insurance industry, State Farm has worked to slow the rate of defection of younger customers to companies such as Progressive and Geico. In one advertising campaign, State Farm emphasizes the potential lost benefit of immediate, personalized service by switching to a less expensive, automated service provider. Finally, a leader can neutralize challengers and slow the rate of defection by attempting to minimize the importance of competitors' benefits. Facebook used this approach as Google entered their social media space more directly with Google+. Facebook has downplayed the benefits of Google+ while continuing to update their presence with features and benefits to enhance their users' experience.

If a new challenger enters your market, the Leader Strategies Matrix provides a means of generating insights on options to maintain and grow the business. As you review the resulting strategic options, be aware of the following turbulence that can jeopardize your status as the market leader:

- Ceding the low end of the market, which potentially leads to ceding the middle of the market as well
- Entering a new market created by the challenger without determining if your core competency and capabilities will translate into success in that market
- Attempting to serve a new customer segment without understanding their unmet needs or jobs to be done
- Not evolving to more profitable points in the value chain when your current point starts to become commoditized
- Trying to add the challenger's new business model onto your current business model
- Ceding a market too quickly to a challenger without fighting when appropriate
- Failure to make trade-offs and trying to be all things to all customers
- Lack of focus, resulting in resources being spread too thin to provide superior value in any one area
- Not leveraging your greater depth of customer insights into ways to help customers become more effective and/or efficient in the jobs they do
- Failure to embed switching costs (e.g., the costs associated with changing brands) into your offerings to keep current customers close
- Trying to launch a new business model using legacy perspectives and ROI metrics

Challenger

A challenger may be a new entrant into the market or one that has maintained a secondary or tertiary position for various reasons. The challenger is often following a first-mover into a market and may face the hurdles of limited brand awareness and fewer resources with which to compete. One of the reasons failure rates for newly launched products are as high as 50 percent is that the challenger sees the market from a product perspective instead of through a customer-need lens. Companies that continually bring "me-too" products to the market not only disappoint potential customers, but also deflate the morale of their salespeople who are left with no differentiated value to sell.

When you find yourself in the role of challenger in a market, consider the following 11 questions to stimulate your thought process and initiate a productive conversation around how to topple the leader:

1. What customer needs or jobs are not currently being fulfilled?
2. Which customer segments are underserved by the leader?
3. Does the leader's offering provide different benefits from our offering?
4. Do the leader's unique benefits include functionality, quality, reliability, convenience, and/or cost?
5. How does the leader's business model differ from ours?
6. What is the leader's value proposition?
7. What is the leader's core competency?
8. What are the leader's top three capabilities?
9. Are we capable of taking away customers from the leader?
10. Are we capable of transforming non-users into customers?
11. In what part of the value chain can we establish a foothold of success in this market?

As you consider these questions, it's important to do so with the mindset of a challenger. I've witnessed managers who have worked on market-leading brands, then moved to challenger brands without adopting an appropriate mindset. A challenger mindset demands the discipline to make real trade-offs and focus one's resources with laser-like precision in only one or two areas that allow them to provide the greatest differentiated value to their targeted customers. It means not whining about a lack of resources and realizing you can't do a little bit of everything in order to play it safe. It means embracing risk and breaking with industry convention to do something that truly stands out.

A moon rocket uses half of its entire fuel supply in the first mile of its journey to generate the momentum necessary to break free of the gravity of the earth's atmosphere. In the same way, a challenger needs to be prepared to invest a large share of its resources breaking targeted customers away from the gravity of the leader's offerings. As the leader rises to that position, they often follow tacit market rules that the industry and customers abide by. In the hotel industry, an 11 a.m. checkout is the norm. In the credit card industry, a late payment finance charge is the norm. In the petroleum industry, gas stations as delivery points for consumer purchases are the norm.

Industry norms mean customers don't have a choice. Industry norms differ from trade-offs in that trade-offs provide customers with a set of options. You can choose X but not Y. You can fly to your destination for an inexpensive fare (low cost), but you'll need to make two connections and have to endure seven hours of layovers (low convenience). It's your choice. But, industry norms offer no choice. So, the ability to creatively think up ways to deviate from industry norms in the favor of customers can provide formidable ways to compete.

Using the Norm Deviation Matrix provides challengers with potential avenues for creating real differentiated value within an established market. Table 2.1 provides a look into how the Norm Deviation Matrix is constructed. In the left column, there are five factors that comprise the customer's experience continuum with a product or service. These factors begin with acquisition and move through use, service, complements, and evolution. The center column lists a market and a particular norm for doing business. In the right column are solutions or ways to deviate from this norm in favor of customers.

For instance, the acquisition factor (purchase/delivery) in the car rental market traditionally had a norm that customers had to go to a car

Table 2.1 Norm Deviation Matrix

Factor	Norm	Solution
Acquisition (purchase/ delivery)	**Auto rentals:** Customers must go to rental agency to pick up rental car.	Enterprise Rent-A-Car will pick you up.
Use	**Movie theaters:** Food is minimal, no alcohol is served, and seating is random.	iPic Theaters introduced high-end food and alcohol in a living-room-like atmosphere with the option of reserved seating.
Service	**Tech support:** Customers must get help via telephone and/or ship computer to distant repair center for fixes.	Apple created the Genius Bar in retail stores for face-to-face computer support.
Complements (other items for use with it)	**Household cleaning:** Bucket, mop, water, and cleaning solution required to clean solid-surface floors.	Swiffer uses easily detachable wet and dry cloths with self-contained cleaning solution.
Evolution (end of use, next use, disposal)	**Vacuums:** Inconvenient purchase, removal, and replacement of bags.	James Dyson developed a bagless vacuum cleaner with a clear receptacle for easy emptying.

rental agency to pick up a rental car. Enterprise Rent-A-Car deviated from that norm by establishing upwards of 90 percent of their locations in communities that enable them to effectively and efficiently provide the option of picking carless customers up. For many years, the norm in the movie theatre market was no alcohol, up-for-grabs seating, and minimal food options. iPic deviated from the use factor norm by introducing higher-end food and alcohol with reserved seating.

To effectively use the Norm Deviation Matrix, identify the norms for each factor on the customer experience continuum, and then think about potential solutions that would deviate from those norms.

In addition to breaking industry norms to create new value for consumers, a challenger's goals may include taking market share from competitors and converting non-users to customers. They can accomplish these goals by creating strategies that leverage their strengths and exploit the competition's weaknesses. Figure 2.2 helps you visually map the Challenger Strategies approach by using the four quadrants of the matrix to develop potential strategies.

When it comes to taking customers from competitors, the challenger can design strategies that change the game, as Cirque du Soleil did when they created a hybrid of the circus and theatre. In this case, Cirque du Soleil effectively took business by creating a new experiential offering for a high-end customer segment that the traditional circus didn't serve.

The challenger can also employ the judo method of positioning a competitor's strengths as weaknesses in order to take some of their customers. A Japanese word for *the gentle way*, judo focuses on using an opponent's strength and weight as weapons against him.[7] As opposed

	Leverage Strengths	Exploit Weaknesses
Take Customers from Competitors	*Change the Game* Take competitors' business by creating or redefining customer segments where your offering can win.	*Judo* Gain competitors' customers by positioning their strengths as weaknesses.
Convert Non-Users to Customers	*Unrealized Potential* Educate non-users on the benefits of adopting your offering.	*Loss Awareness* Create urgency in non-users regarding the opportunity costs of not utilizing your offerings.

Figure 2.2   Challenger Strategies

to resisting the force of the opponent, you go with it and twist it to your advantage. This was the approach that retailer Target took as they implied that Walmart every day low prices would limit the style quotient of their products versus Target's chic value offerings.

A challenger can also leverage strengths to convert non-users to customers. Here, you're educating potential customers not currently engaged in the market on the benefits of your offering. Before being purchased by Microsoft, Skype was successful in educating non-users on the benefits of video calling. In many cases, Skype offered free video calling—even overseas. While initially carving out space in the business market, Skype also found success in the family and friends market, allowing people who were miles away to maintain relationships and *see* one another.

Another method for converting non-users to customers is to create a sense of urgency in those not participating in the market's offerings by letting them know what they're missing. Match.com, an online dating website, used this loss-awareness strategy to show single people that they just may miss meeting their soul mate by not becoming a member. As a challenger, can you illustrate the opportunity costs of not using your offerings? Research by Nobel Prize winner Daniel Kahneman and Amos Tversky has demonstrated that people are more motivated by the thought of losing something than by an equivalent gain.[8] Therefore, positioning your offering's benefits as preventing a loss (missing out on a life with your soul mate) versus attaining the equivalent gain (finding your soul mate) has a significant influence on a potential customer's decision-making process.

The Challenger Strategies Matrix provides underdogs with a way to explore methods for profitably growing the business by taking customers from the leader or converting non-users into customers. As you review these potential strategies, be aware of the following turbulence that can stall your upward challenger trajectory:

- Playing the same game as the market leader
- Failure to overcommit resources at the decisive point
- Staying within the industry and market rules

- Reacting to the actions of the market leader or other challengers
- Getting drawn into the product-feature war of bells and whistles
- Lack of focus on the target customer's most important needs and jobs to be done
- Not understanding which specific customer segments find the most value in what you offer
- Allowing the market leader to remain comfortable
- Trying to capture all of the market at once
- Failure to shock the market out of the status quo
- Not determining the profitable point of the value chain where you can provide differentiated value

Spectator

Many products and services continue to receive time and budget each year without providing much value to customers or profit to the company. These spectators either mindlessly react to the competition's moves, or they sit passively by and watch competitors continue to grow at their expense. A manager, by the very definition of the term, is someone who has control of and responsibility for the direction of their business. An important but often neglected part of this responsibility is to disengage from offerings, markets, and customers that are no longer providing value and profits to the organization. During his tenure as CEO of Exxon Mobil, Lee Raymond had a requirement that 3 to 5 percent of the company's assets be identified for disengagement every year.[9] Having this type of requirement in place can reawaken people's mindset and discipline to make real trade-offs.

In my experience providing strategic counsel to senior leaders around the world, there are two types of disengagement: active and passive. Active disengagement involves reviewing areas of resource allocation on a monthly basis and jettisoning activities, projects, reports, and tactics that are either are not working or not providing value. As noted earlier, research has shown that the number-one driver of revenue growth is the reallocation of resources from underperforming initiatives to those with greater promise.[10] However, because in most organizations strategic planning is an annual event rather than an ongoing dialogue of key business issues, passive disengagement is much more common. In passive disengagement, managers tend to wait for planning season to arrive to make changes. And typically, the changes they make aren't significant enough to make a difference. A study of more than 1,500 companies over a 15-year period showed that a full one-third of businesses received almost exactly the amount of capital in a given year as they did the year before.[11]

Are all the hours your team invests in the strategic planning process resulting in significant changes in resource allocation? For most leaders, there are changes in their market, changes in customer value drivers, and changes in the competitive landscape from year to year. Yet, the areas they allocate resources to and the corresponding amounts see little, if any, change. Unless you as a leader are involved in active disengagement on a regular basis, you are most likely wasting a significant portion of your people's time and budget. As Twitter co-founder Evan Williams said, "When I meet with the founders of a new company, my advice is almost always, 'Do fewer things.' The vast majority of things are distractions and very few really matter to your success."[12] The discipline to do fewer things—to focus—begins with your ability to disengage.

If you find your product or service in a spectator role, it's time to honestly answer the following five questions:

1. Why are we in this category?
2. Is this offering contributing profits to the business?
3. How can we redesign or reposition the offering so that it brings unique value to key customers, resulting in greater profit?
4. Would the customers we value most miss this offering if we discontinued it?
5. Could we bring more value to the market if we discontinued this offering and focused our resources on more profitable offerings?

Taking into account your position in the market when developing strategy means it's conditional. Not taking into account your position in the market when developing strategy means you're ripe for getting beat. Are you a leader, challenger, or spectator? Who are you, and what are you going to do about it?

Competitive Advantage

While it's been debated how long a company can sustain competitive advantage in a market, the aim of most firms is to deliver superior value to their customers in a profitable way. Research shows that the primary means to profitably deliver superior value is through differentiation. A study involving 25,000 companies over a 40-year period demonstrated that the firms achieving the highest return on assets delivered superior value because of their positive differentiation.[13] Another study of 200 companies showed that 93 percent of the top 20 percent of financial performers have a strong form of differentiation in their core, which led to competitive advantage in their market.[14] Differentiation enables a firm to charge a premium price relative to competitive offerings, operate at a lower cost than competitors, or, potentially, both. As ESPN president John Skipper said, "If you are going to compete, you have to have points of difference. There is no value coming into the market and doing the same thing."[15]

Creating, developing, or discovering real differentiation that fuels the delivery of superior value takes time, thought, and the courage to make trade-offs with one's resources. The intellectually lazy leader's shortcut of offering similar products or services in the same way as competitors, only trying to do it slightly better, does not constitute differentiation. It's common to hear these people complain that the products or services their research and development group have come up with don't offer any differentiation. Look, if people selling bottled water can find ways to create differentiation, then so can you. One could argue that bottled still water is as close to a commodity as you could find. So, following that logic, all bottled water producers should have the same market share, right? Wrong. According to market research firm Information Resources Inc., Nestle Water Pure Life had a 10 percent market share in the still waters category as of May

2012 while Poland Springs was at 6 percent.[16] As former Harvard Business School professor Theodore Levitt wrote, "One thing is certain: there is no such thing as a commodity—or, at least from a competitive point of view, there need not be. Everything is differentiable, and, in fact, usually is differentiated. All goods and services are differentiable."[17]

A majority of leaders deceive themselves into thinking they've cultivated valuable differentiation. A study conducted by Bain & Company surveyed executives and their customers on the level of differentiation they believed the offerings possessed. The researchers concluded, "We found that while 80 percent of executives felt their offering was highly differentiated, only about 8 percent of their customers actually agreed with them."[18] True differentiated value isn't determined by you. It is determined by your customer, and it shows up in the form of your profits.

Competitive advantage can be defined then as the ability to deliver superior value based on differentiation rooted in capabilities. Capabilities are comprised of resources and activities that are competitively relevant. Capabilities are what you do (activities) with what you have (resources). Competitive advantage isn't defined as having the best product or a better service, because in the end, best and better are subjective, depending on the customer and the type of value they seek. Harvard Business School professor Michael Porter echoed these sentiments when he said, "There is no best auto company, there is no best car. You're really competing to be unique. . . . Whole Foods Markets is not just trying to be a great food retailer. It's trying to meet the needs of a certain set of customers."[19]

One of the areas that surprises experienced senior leadership teams when they participate in my strategy development workshops is their lack of meaningful insights about the competition. In working with a highly successful mobile technology leadership team based in Latin America whose members averaged more than 20 years of industry experience each, they were unable to clearly and concisely articulate their competitor's strategic approach to the market. They knew many facts about their competitors, things like locations, head count, service areas, contracting approaches, and product specifications, but facts are different than insights. Insights are created by the ability to piece together previously unrelated bits of information—to connect the dots—uncovering the competitor's strategic intent and their relative advantage or disadvantage in the market.

A tool that may be helpful in determining a competitor's strategic intent is the Competitive Advantage Profile. The Competitive Advantage Profile is a concise, yet comprehensive way to understand whether you have an advantage, disadvantage, or are at parity—and most important, why. Table 2.2 is the Competitive Advantage Profile template that can be used to break down the competition to more thoroughly understand the foundation on which they attempt to outperform you. The tool is a simple method of aggregating insights in eight areas that have been previously reviewed.

Table 2.2   Competitive Advantage Profile

	You:	Competitor:	Competitor:
Position (Competitive condition)			
Core competency (Area of expertise)			
Capabilities (Resources/ activities)			
Customer (Who they target)			
Need (Job they fulfill)			
Approach (How they deliver value)			
Benefits (Advantages)			
Value proposition (Message)			

The position describes a company's competitive condition, its current place in the market: leader, challenger, or spectator. As you discuss the position, you'll want to first determine what benchmark or metric you'll be using to describe the competitive condition (e.g., market share, revenue, sales volume, profit, etc.). This conversation should include some preliminary discussion around why the competitor holds that position. If they are a leader, try to determine what has driven them to that spot: first-mover advantage, superior intellectual property, favored brand, and so on. Once you've moved through the remainder of the Competitive Advantage Profile, the answer to why they hold their particular position should become clear.

The second element in the Competitive Advantage Profile is the core competency. As you'll recall from the previous description in the Coalesce discipline section, a core competency is the primary area of expertise. It's the collective learning of a group residing in their knowledge, skills, and technology. A core competency is the know-how that serves as the foundation for their ability to deliver value in a competitively superior way. Examples of company core competencies include Berkshire Hathaway's analysis, Nordstrom's customer satisfaction, and Disney's creativity.

The third component of the Competitive Advantage Profile is capability. A capability is an organization's potential for using its resources to carry out specific activities to create value. Capabilities refer to the competitively relevant activities performed with key resources to drive the strategy's success. Examples of capabilities include Nike's brand management, Marvel Comics' repurposing of content (e.g., transitioning comic book characters into action movie stars), and Nerf's product development. Keep in mind that capabilities are the competitively relevant activities, meaning those that use resources in a way that creates differentiated value for the business.

Since competitive advantage is defined as "the ability to deliver superior value . . .," it is important to see exactly how their approach to value and your approach to value match up. The remainder of the

Competitive Advantage Profile breaks down the value proposition into its discrete elements. The fourth component is the customer, who the business is specifically targeting with their offerings. The fifth component is the customer's unmet need or job-to-be-done. The sixth element is the approach the company is taking in how they are going to uniquely fulfill the unmet need or job-to-be-done. The seventh element is the benefit provided to the customer by using a competitor's offering. And finally, the eighth element is the summarized value proposition, or message to the market on why customers should choose one offering over the other potential options. It's helpful to begin this exercise by completing the first column with your profile, which can later be used to compare to key competitors in order to identify differences that lead to either advantage or disadvantage.

A more thorough understanding of the dynamic of competitive advantage in your market will play a vital role in crafting future strategy. A study of 2,135 global leaders showed that only 53 percent would describe their firms' strategies as focusing on the development of advantage versus their competitors. The remainder characterized their strategies as simply matching industry best practices and maintaining operational standards.[20] It can be argued that competitive advantage is fleeting. It can be argued that your source of competitive advantage will sooner or later be copied. But it cannot be argued that you should constantly strive to deliver superior value to customers; in other words, creating competitive advantage.

Competitive Intelligence

Complete the following five sentences about your spouse, partner, or significant other:

1. His/her favorite flavor of ice cream is . . .
2. The name of the high school he/she attended is . . .
3. His/her favorite musician or band is . . .
4. His/her favorite food is . . .
5. His/her pants size is . . .

Ok, so maybe pants size wasn't fair. How did you do? How many of the answers were you absolutely sure of? After all, they are arguably the closest person to you in your life. Did you get all five? Really?

I led a strategy program with an organization that was the leader in their market. For the dozen senior executives in the room, the average length of industry experience was 23 years. After two days of strategic thinking exercises on the industry, customers, competitors, and their organization, one of the main conclusions they arrived at was this: "Coming into the session, we figured we knew everything there is to know about the business. What amazed us the most is how little we really know about the competition." And this is from a market leader who had performed exceptionally well during the past five years, but was beginning to lose share to the competition.

As we saw in the personal partner quiz, just because you occupy the same physical space doesn't necessarily mean you know everything you potentially should about your loved one. The same can be said for competition. Just because you occupy the same market space doesn't mean you know all the critical things about them that can help you develop strategy to deliver greater value to customers. As you worked through the Competitive Advantage Profile in the previous section, there may have been some things you simply didn't know. This lack of awareness can have very real consequences for your business. A survey of 1,825 senior executives found that "only 23 percent learned about a competitor's new product launch early enough to respond before it hit the market, and only 12 percent learned about a price change in time."[21]

One of the questions I often receive during the strategic thinking programs I lead is: "How can we possibly be expected to know all of this information about our competitors, especially, if they're private companies?" My response is generally: "You may not know it, but your prospective customers will when they are deciding between your offering and the competitor's offering." The differences in the areas of investment and the value delivered by you and your competitors are the factors on which they'll most likely be basing their decision.

Here are three introductory steps for ramping up competitive intelligence efforts:

1. **Question:** The first step to ensuring you have strong competitive intelligence is to pose questions to your team. An effective means of posing these questions is to utilize a strategy survey prior to an off-site strategic thinking session. This enables managers to devote time and thoughtfully consider the key business issues from their perspective without the immediate influence of others. Not giving people time to develop their thoughts individually either prior to the meeting or during the meeting results in a chain reaction of comments based on the first statement, instead of a range of individual viewpoints. It's important to structure the session with a methodical and comprehensive set of questions and tools to stimulate thinking in order to explore the competitive landscape fully. Following are a sample of questions that can catalyze the discussion:

   o Who is your most dangerous competitor and why?

   o What are potential substitutes for your offering that are not direct competitors, but can perform the same function?

   o Which of the following indirect competition is having the biggest impact on your profitability: suppliers, customers, substitutes, or the status quo?

   o What are the top five factors of competition in your market: the places where you invest to win (e.g., sales force, marketing, IT, product innovation, etc.)?

   o Keeping in mind those top five factors of competition, what is your relative resource allocation (time, people, budget) versus the competition for each factor?

   o What is the quantitative value your offerings provide to customers relative to that of the competition?

   o What are the top three reasons you've lost business to competitors in the past year?

2. **Link:** During the competitive discussion, numerous insights will be uncovered that can have a dramatically positive impact on the business. Not only will you want to visually capture those insights using competitive models, you'll also want to link the competitive insights with customer and market insights. Additionally, an objective look at your internal capabilities is crucial in establishing realistic competitive positioning moving forward. Completing the Competitive Advantage Profile provides a concise way to capture people's thinking on the key aspects of the competitive landscape.

3. **Act:** Develop communication channels for your frontline people (sales, business development, managers), across functional areas and up through levels. This ensures the people with the greatest access to new competitive insights have the ability to share what they learn with others in the organization. This enhances everyone's decision making because strategy and tactics should never be set in a vacuum. It also informs your team members that strategy is everyone's job. Educate people at all levels as to what insights are and how to share those insights, reminding them that strategy is indeed their job. The beginning of the definition of strategy is, "the intelligent allocation of limited resources. . . ." Everyone has resources, including time, talent, and budget. How they choose to use their resources will determine the company's real strategy and ultimately, their success or failure.

Trade-Off Zone

Good strategy inherently involves trade-offs: choosing one path and not the other. Competitors trying to be all things to all people are the easiest to beat. The mark of a great company is that their trade-offs result in extreme focus, enabling them to carve out a distinct position in consumers' awareness. Mention a great company's name and one thing will immediately come to mind: their distinct position (e.g., Walmart = low prices). Say a mediocre company's name and you're left searching for their position, usually winding up with nothing more than their general market category. To compete at an optimal level demands the discipline to make trade-offs. Oftentimes, these trade-offs involve things that your competitors cannot or will not do. As former world chess champion Garry Kasparov said, "What separates a winner from a loser at the grandmaster level is the willingness to do the unthinkable. A brilliant strategy is, certainly, a matter of intelligence, but intelligence without audaciousness is not enough. I must have the guts to explode the game, to upend my opponent's thinking and, in so doing, unnerve him."[22]

A tool that can be used to help gauge your trade-offs relative to the competition is the Trade-Off Zone. The Trade-Off Zone is a visual representation of the trade-offs, or lack thereof, being made in a market. The tool identifies five common trade-off factors, and additional factors can be added if they figure prominently in the customer's value equation. The five primary benefit factors are quality, convenience, cost, service, and selection. Competitors are plotted in the low, medium, or high zone for each factor based on their performance delivering that particular benefit. Figure 2.3 provides an example of the Trade-Off Zone.

To construct a Trade-Off Zone for your business, first select the specific type of customer that the offering is targeting. In some cases, the root of poor strategy is trying to be all things to all customers. If some potential customers are not happy with how you're choosing to bring

	Low	Medium	High
Quality			
Convenience			
Cost			
Service			
Selection			

Figure 2.3   Trade-Off Zone

value to the market, it's a sign that trade-offs have been made. The point is that effective strategy is going to upset some potential customers, be they internal or external customers. Learn to live with it. Just as a real leader isn't going to please all followers, a real strategy isn't going to please all customers.

The manager then rates their offering for each of the trade-off factors as low, medium, or high, as seen by the targeted customer. Competitive offerings are then plotted, creating trade-off profiles, to determine where differentiation exists within the Trade-Off Zone. If your trade-off profile mirrors the competition, work needs to be done to determine the trade-off factors targeted customers value, and how to create positive differentiation around them.

Figure 2.4 provides an example of the Trade-Off Zone for three fictitious technology companies, representing the three different value disciplines: TechnoStar (product leadership), CustoSolution (customer intimacy), and CostAlert (operational excellence).

Using the Trade-Off Zone, it becomes apparent which benefit factors each company is using to steer customers to their offering. Customers

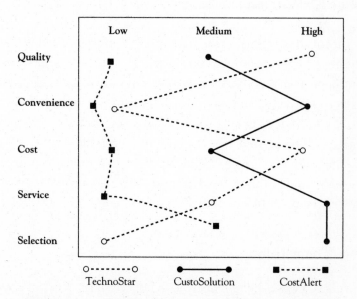

Figure 2.4   Trade-Off Zone for Three Companies

with a greater demand for quality would be more likely to choose TechnoStar, while those customers more interested in cost savings would prefer CostAlert. Those wanting higher service and selection would prefer CustoSolution. Based on the value discipline your company invests a disproportionate amount of resources into, the resulting trade-off profile should show points of difference among the benefit factors. If you are bringing differentiated value to customers, this will be reflected in differences in the Trade-Off Zone. If your offering is at parity, you'll see competitive convergence or a mirroring of trade-off profiles with your competition.

The following questions can start your thinking about the Trade-Off Zone:

- Which specific customer types are you choosing to serve?
- Which potential customer types are you choosing not to serve?
- Which benefit factors does your targeted customer most value?
- Which of the trade-off factors are you able to provide the most differentiated value to your targeted customers?
- Which benefit factors are you not going to focus on?

As you construct the Trade-Off Zone for your business, keep in mind your desired target customer. The way you configure your trade-offs will not appeal to everyone. Therefore, you must have a clear picture of the factors of value that are most relevant to your target customer. In fact, if you've developed a sound strategy built on legitimate trade-offs, there will be certain types of potential customers who won't like your configuration of trade-offs at all. This is a difficult concept for some leaders to wrap their head around. "Are you saying some potential customers won't like us at all?" Yes.

Indirect Competition

Coke versus Pepsi. Nike versus Adidas. Google versus Facebook. When we think competition, we think rivals. However, the true intent of business competition is not to beat the opponent. The real goal is to earn greater profits for the company. The battle for these profits is fought on multiple fronts, only one of which is with direct rivals. The indirect competitors for profits include customers, suppliers, potential entrants, and producers of substitutes. Michael Porter described these players and their interaction with one another as the Five Forces of Competition.[23] Porter wrote, "The point of industry analysis is not to declare the industry attractive or unattractive but to understand the underpinnings of competition and the root causes of profitability. Understanding the forces that shape industry competition is the starting point for developing strategy. The five forces reveal why industry profitability is what it is."[24]

While direct rivals consume most of the mind share of leaders, it's the indirect competitors that can quietly eat away at your profits and position in the industry value chain. As professors Bergen and Peteraf write, "Among those competitors that possess equivalent resources, indirect competitors pose the strongest threat to a focal company."[25] To more fully understand how these indirect competitors influence your business, the following sets of questions have been developed for each type of indirect competitor: customers, suppliers, potential entrants, and substitutes.

When considering *customers* and their effect on your portion of profits, the following questions may be helpful:

- Have we been able to raise prices in the past in order to secure a greater share of profits? Why or why not?
- Have we cultivated the perception of differentiated value in the minds of customers for our offerings?
- Are there switching costs for customers to overcome in transitioning from one offering to another within the market?
- Is there any indication our customers would integrate backwards into our part of the industry value chain?
- What is the size of our customer's margins and how much pressure is there on those margins?

When considering *suppliers* and their effect on your portion of profits, the following questions may be helpful:

- Have we been able to obtain price decreases from our suppliers in the past two years? Why or why not?
- How many potential suppliers are in the market that could readily fulfill our needs?
- What percentage of our supplier's business do we represent?
- Is there any indication our suppliers would integrate forward into our position in the industry value chain?
- What is the size of our supplier's margins and how much pressure is there on those margins?

When considering *potential entrants* and their effect on your portion of profits, the following questions may be helpful:

- Has there been an influx of new competitors into our market in the past two years? Why or why not?
- What is the threshold level of capital and intellectual property required to successfully enter our market?
- Is our market susceptible to disruptive innovation in the form of a simpler, low-cost, more convenient offering with an enabling technology that appeals to greater segments of customers?
- Do economies of scale serve as an advantage and barrier to entry in this market?
- What unmet customer needs or jobs to be done could a new entrant fulfill?

When considering *substitutes* and their effect on your portion of profits, the following questions may be helpful:

- Have there been any substitutes entering the market in the past two years? If so, what unmet needs have they filled and how successful have they been?

- What potential offerings not currently used in this market could perform a function that would fulfill customer's needs?
- Have we established any switching costs that would stop or slow the defection of current customers to a substitute's offering?
- Which part of the market would be most ripe for a substitute to enter? Why?
- Could we establish a tiered offering from a functionality, convenience, or cost perspective that would effectively combat a substitute offering?

Intangible Competition

In addition to direct and indirect competitors, there is also the effect of intangible competition on a company's profits. Intangible competition by its very nature involves factors that you can't see or touch. These factors have an effect on your profits, yet aren't included in the groups of direct and indirect competitors. Intangible competition includes affinity for the status quo, apathy, and priorities.

The status quo represents the existing state of affairs. An affinity for the status quo is a human condition where people tend to favor the way things are versus potential change. This is understandable in that change requires effort. It requires people to both think and act differently. New thinking and new action may in turn induce anxiety and discomfort, as well as expose us to risk and potential failure. It's no wonder then we prefer the status quo to change.

What is puzzling is why people prefer the status quo when the existing state of affairs is not favorable or the change would lead to an improved situation. In a review of several studies of patients undergoing heart surgery, the results showed that despite a new opportunity for greater health and longevity following the procedure, the majority of patients didn't follow their doctor's recommendations to change their lifestyle. Instead, they opted for the status quo. Dr. Edward Miller, dean of the medical school and chief executive officer of the hospital at Johns Hopkins University, explains: "If you look at people after coronary-artery bypass grafting two years later, 90 percent have not changed their lifestyle. And that's been studied over and over again. Even though they know they have a very bad disease and they know they should change their lifestyle, for whatever reason, they can't."[26]

An affinity for the status quo exists within your organization and externally with your customers. Internally, the affinity for the status quo manifests itself during the strategic planning process as managers continue to allocate their resources in virtually the same way year after year. Failing to include strategic thinking sessions prior to the planning part of the process results in no new thinking and no new insights. Without new insights about the market, customers, competitors or the company, there's no catalyst for change. And that's why most strategic plans look the same year in and year out, and generate little if any incremental growth.

A customer's affinity for the status quo is a formidable competitor. When you introduce a new product or service, in most cases you're asking customers to make changes in their thinking and behavior. Then you're hoping they sustain those changes over time. As the heart surgery studies indicated, making and maintaining changes, even when they could mean the difference between life and death, is rare. This is why leaders who find themselves in the role of challenger to a market leader need to overcommit resources and focus like a laser in one area. It's this type of over-the-top effort that's demanded in order to break customers out of the status quo.

Several questions to consider in overcoming the affinity for the status quo as it relates to your business issue:

- How would you describe the status quo?
- What are all of the potential alternatives to the status quo?
- What is the most compelling reason the other party would consider moving out of the status quo?
- What behavioral modifications are required for change?
- What tools, techniques, or support would facilitate lasting change?

Apathy is another intangible competitor that can put a dent in the attempt to grow profits. Apathy is described as a lack of interest or excitement in something that others may be passionate about. Apathy is indifference to the product, service, event, person, or situation at hand. Leaders are faced with internal apathy when too many flavor-of-the-month initiatives are thoughtlessly rolled out, one after the other. This occurs within the context of strategy, when leaders fail to take the time to share with employees what the strategy means to them, why it was developed, and how it translates to their daily work. I refer to this as the 10 Commandment Approach to Strategy. The 10 Commandment approach occurs when leaders spend 45 minutes rolling through their strategic-plan PowerPoint presentation and then indirectly proclaim, "Now go forth and strategize," assuming their work communicating the strategy is done.

Apathy is also encountered by salespeople in their interaction with customers. When they attempt to sell products or services that weren't developed with insights into customer's unmet needs, their me-too offering is met with a blank look that screams, "Who cares?" Certainly, good salespeople still find a way to make the sale, perhaps by leveraging their relationship with the customer, bundling the offering with more desired products, or planting seeds of doubt about the competitor's offering. However, the customer's apathy could have been avoided altogether if the business's product development, research, or marketing departments had focused on differentiated value for the target customer to begin with.

Several questions to consider in overcoming apathy as it relates to your business issue are:

- What is the cause of apathy?
- What is the extent or reach of the apathy?
- What factors are involved in the apathy?
- What is the full range of options for altering the apathy?
- Are there any solutions for moving out of apathy we could take from other industries, organizations, or situations and apply here?

Another barrier to greater profitability are priorities that differ or are not aligned. Internally, priorities can prove to be an intangible competitor because different groups are often tasked with different goals. It's not uncommon for one brand team to garner a greater share of their sales force's time in the field based on the structure of the incentive compensation plan. Based on the weight of the incentive compensation plan, some brand teams may find that their priorities (selling more of brand X) don't even match up with the priorities of their *own* sales force (selling more of brand Y because that's where they'll make more money). Internal priorities can also differ from the global to the national to the regional to the district levels. In my strategy work with several Fortune 500 companies, I've heard more than a few times that the North American leadership team can't pursue the best strategic course in the United States because leaders at their global headquarters in Europe won't support it.

The external challenge with competing priorities can be seen when companies are not truly driven by fulfilling customers' unmet needs. Instead, they work off their own internal agenda and hope it somehow meshes with the customers' agenda so they can be considered strategic partners. Unless an organization has taken the time to observe customers, identify their key jobs to be done, and produced solutions that deliver differentiated value on those unmet needs, the term strategic partner is a farce. While customers may not always be able to articulate their priorities, strategic leaders are able to infer how their organization can deliver superior value based on differentiation grounded in their capabilities.

Several questions to consider in overcoming priorities as it relates to your business issue are:

- What are the priorities of the other groups we work with internally?
- Are our priorities and the priorities of these other internal groups aligned?
- Have we identified our key customers' top priorities?

- Have we identified our key customers' unmet needs or jobs to be done?
- How can we align our goals and priorities with our customers' priorities and unmet needs?

A study of more than 3,000 global executives showed that the biggest business challenge leaders face is innovating to achieve competitive differentiation in their market.[27] Competition is all around us. Your ability to assess, understand, and outperform the various types of competition will influence your organization's trajectory. Competition involves striving together, reaching for higher levels of performance. Those higher levels of performance are directly related to your insights for providing customers with differentiated value. Compete, strive, and reach your full potential.

1,000-Foot View

The term compete comes from the Latin *competere* meaning "to strive together."

Three competitive conditions a business may find itself in are: leader, challenger, or spectator.

The Leader Strategies Matrix provides options for protecting one's business and systematically exploring new routes to profitable growth.

The Norm Deviation Matrix provides challengers with potential avenues for creating real differentiated value within an established market by examining tacit market rules that can be changed to their advantage.

The Challenger Strategies Matrix provides options for taking customers from leaders or converting non-users to users.

Competitive advantage is the ability to deliver superior value based on differentiation rooted in capabilities.

The Competitive Advantage Profile is a tool for assessing which player in the market possesses competitive advantage and why.

The Trade-Off Zone is a visual representation of the trade-offs, or lack of trade-offs, being made in a market.

Indirect competitors for profits include customers, suppliers, potential entrants, and producers of substitutes.

Intangible competition includes affinity for the status quo, apathy, and priorities.

Champion

*When challenge and adversity are all around,
only then is a champion found.*

R esting in the Horn of Africa, Somalia was engulfed in a brutal civil war and widespread famine in 1993. A peacekeeping effort by the United Nations was under attack and valiant members of the United States Army Rangers and Delta Force soldiers were deployed to capture the Somali warlord leading the attack. Also assisting in the effort was the United States Army 160th Special Operations Aviation Regiment (Airborne), known as the Night Stalkers. During the Battle of Mogadishu, two Night Stalker Black Hawk helicopters, Super Six One and Super Six Four, were shot down. As described in the book by Mark Bowden with the movie of the same name, *Black Hawk Down*, 19 brave American soldiers gave their lives in service of the country. The heroic soldiers involved in this event demonstrated the ultimate example of what it means *to champion*: to fight for, protect, defend, and support.

While many of us will never know that level of service in a life and death arena, we can in a different context strive to champion the direction of our organizations. To effectively champion a group's strategic direction could very well mean the difference between success or bankruptcy and employment or unemployment for thousands of people. Developing a strong strategy means that you've made trade-offs, and trade-offs mean that some of your potential customers aren't going to be happy. While we know good strategy is not going to please all potential external customers, what's often overlooked is that good strategy is also going to upset some of your internal customers as well. Moving resources (time, people, and budget) from one area to another is sure to stir up emotions as some people will see the changes as hurting their ability to run their part of the business. Therefore, any good strategy will come under attack internally because of the changes it causes. And when the strategy comes under attack, you'll need to defend, or champion it. In championing the strategy, a disciplined approach to managing time, influencing others and continually developing new skills will be critical to success.

Using Time Strategically

Time is the coin of your life. It is the only coin you have, and only you can determine how it will be spent. Be careful lest you let other people spend it for you.

—Carl Sandburg, American poet and
Pulitzer Prize-winning writer

As one's leadership responsibilities increase, their disposable time can decrease proportionately. More meetings, more e-mail, seemingly more of everything multiplies and eats up time. A survey of 1,500 leaders on their time allocation showed that only 9 percent were "very satisfied" with how they spend their time and nearly 50 percent confessed that they didn't spend enough time on strategic direction.[1] As leaders move to higher levels in an organization, it's natural for them to continue applying their expertise to a wide variety of operational and tactical issues that arise, even if those issues are no longer within their realm of responsibility. A three-year study of 39 companies in eight industries found that, on average, 41 percent of a manager's time is consumed by these discretionary activities that could and should be handled by others.[2] While performing these unnecessary types of tasks is a natural inclination, it also does them a disservice in the long run. Their inability to let go of past tasks results in not cultivating new skills that will be instrumental to the firm's future success and it hinders the development of other managers who should be fulfilling these responsibilities.

Leaders who are unable to delegate often rely more heavily on multitasking. One of the main ingredients in the multitasking recipe is e-mail. It's estimated that the average manager spends approximately 23 percent of their day on e-mail, with one analysis calculating the time on e-mail at nearly 50 percent.[3,4] It's not uncommon to observe a leader in a meeting reviewing and responding to e-mails on one of their devices while potentially important insights are shared by others and missed by them. A 10-year study of thousands of managers found that 40 percent continually work in a distracted state, characterized by a lack of focus and their mistaking activity for achievement.[5] If the people and topics in a meeting don't deserve your undivided attention, then why are you there in the first place?

While working on several things at once may provide a feeling of overachievement, it's in fact a smokescreen for lower productivity. As researchers in a *Harvard Business Review* study concluded, "You may suspect that multitasking is counterproductive and new data suggest it is. The more workers switch tasks, the less they accomplish."[6] Citing a cumulative body of scientific research, authors Derek Dean and Caroline Webb conclude:

> *Multitasking makes human beings less productive, less creative, and less able to make good decisions. If we want to be effective leaders, we need to stop. . . . When we switch between tasks, especially complex ones, we become startlingly less efficient: participants who completed tasks in parallel took up to 30 percent longer and made twice as many errors as those who completed the same tasks in sequence.[7]*

Leaders lacking a disciplined approach to applying their expertise and time can also become meeting magnets, where they are pulled into far more meetings than they actually should attend. One study showed that 60 percent of a CEO's time is consumed by meetings.[8] Unfortunately, all meetings are not created equal. Executives at the highest performing companies spend half their time in decision-making meetings and less than 10 percent of their time in report-driven informational meetings.[9] Think back on the meetings you attended this past week: What percentage of these meetings were focused on decision-making and what percentage were purely report-driven and informational?

Perhaps this is why nearly half of all leaders surveyed concluded that the way the spend their time does not really match up with the organization's strategic priorities.[10] If you're constantly being pulled into meetings without firm decision-making intent or an agenda not aligned with key priorities, you're wasting precious time. As management guru Peter Drucker noted, "Time is the scarcest resource, and unless it is managed, nothing else can be managed."

As a leader's responsibilities increase, so too does the need for individual think time. LinkedIn CEO Jeff Weiner explains the transition:

> There will always be a need to get things done and knock another To-Do item off the list. However, as the company grows larger, as the breadth and depth of your initiatives expand, and as the competitive and technological landscape continues to shift at an accelerating rate—you will require more time than ever before to just think. That thinking, if done properly, requires uninterrupted focus. . . . In other words, it takes time. And that time will only be available if you carve it out for yourself.[11]

For those with an "activity = achievement" mindset, this is a particularly challenging idea. However, in a study of more than 1,000 executives, the number-one response of how highly satisfied leaders invest their time was "alone."[12] Unfortunately, additional research shows that only 11 percent of a CEO's time is spent alone.[13] The great leaders don't hope this individual think time magically appears on their calendars. They make it happen. LinkedIn CEO Weiner shares his approach to making think time happen:

> If you were to see my calendar, you'd probably notice a host of time slots greyed out but with no indication of what's going on. . . . The grey sections reflect "buffers," or time periods I've purposely kept clear of meetings. In aggregate, I schedule between 90 minutes and two hours of these buffers every day (broken into 30- to 90-minute blocks). It's a system I developed over the last several years in response to a schedule that was becoming so jammed with back-to-back meetings that I had little time left to process what was going on around me or just think.[14]

Ranked the number-one CEO in the world by *Forbes Magazine* in 2012, Amazon.com CEO Jeff Bezos is also a believer in individual think time. He uses a quarterly solo retreat as a way to transform thinking into new value for customers. Amazon's fulfillment center for third-party sellers is just one example of the innovations that his individual think time has generated. Bezos said, "I just lock myself up. There are no distractions from the office. No phones ringing. It's just because with a little bit of isolation I find I start to get more creative."[15]

Why then, don't most leaders create individual think time? An Economist Intelligence Unit survey of 377 executives found that two-thirds of leaders in the bottom-performing companies cited the challenge: "We are too busy fighting the daily battle to step back."[16] When your team becomes too busy to stop and think about the business, prepare the lifeboats because there's obviously more time being spent rearranging the proverbial deck chairs than getting important tasks accomplished.

The other reason individual think time is often overlooked is because the organization already has a strategic planning process in place. Leadership assumes that all of the thinking will take place during the scheduled time. The reality is that there is often lots of process and little new thinking. A process driven by the goal of filling out templates rather than generating new insights is doomed from the start. Tesla Motors and SpaceX founder Elon Musk said, "The problem is that at a lot of big companies, process becomes a substitute for thinking."[17] The key is to carve out time for both individual and group thinking on a continual basis to ensure you're harnessing insights in a proactive manner.

Time Trade-Off Techniques

To more effectively utilize time in your leadership role, consider the following three ideas:

1. **Dedicate chunks of time to a single task**. The opposite of multitasking is to work on one task at a time—simple in concept, challenging to practice. Dedicating a significant portion of time to one task can boost productivity in two important ways. First, setting time aside to focus on one thing increases productivity by as much as 65 percent in some studies because the person

is able to channel all of their cognitive processing power to a single item.[18] Second, focusing on one task and not allowing any interruptions prevents those interruptions from wasting valuable time getting back to the original task. Research has shown that people take on average, 24 minutes to return to the original task after an interruption.[19] Start blocking out 30-minute chunks of time to dedicate to single tasks.

2. **Send fewer e-mails**. While it can be difficult to limit the number of e-mails you receive, you do have influence over how many e-mails you send. One company's total e-mail output dropped by 54 percent over a three-month period after the company's leaders reduced the number of e-mails they sent out. The company realized a gain of 10,400 man-hours over the course of the year, all started by executives limiting the number of e-mails they sent to others.[20]

3. **Make time trade-offs**. Before we can improve on a current state, we need to understand what the current state is. If we're going to improve our ability to allocate time effectively, then we first need to determine where our time is currently being spent. The following steps will help you improve your time allocation:

Step 1: For a typical week, record how you spend your time in 30-minute increments throughout the day.

Step 2: After the week has elapsed, identify the time categories (e.g., operational meetings, e-mail, teleconferences, customer meetings, etc.). For each category, list the total amount of time invested during the week.

Step 3: Label the time categories and increments of time on the Time Gauge graph (Figure 3.1).

Step 4: Plot the time investments for each category and connect the dots for your current investment.

Step 5: Review the Time Gauge results and then use the Time Trade-Off Matrix to place the investment categories in either the "Eliminate," "Decrease," or "Increase" quadrant depending on how you'd like to change that particular category investment. Fill the "Create" quadrant with any new areas you'd like to invest time.

Step 6: Plot the ideal time investments for each category based on the results of the Time Trade-Off Matrix and connect the dots using a dashed line to represent your "ideal" investment.

Step 7: Record the action steps necessary to achieve the ideal time investment.

Figure 3.1 is an example of a Time Gauge for a senior executive. On the x-axis are listed the areas of investment such as operational meetings, teleconferences, and metrics review. On the y-axis is the actual amount of time invested per week into those activities. In this case, very little time is being spent on strategy and solitary planning time,

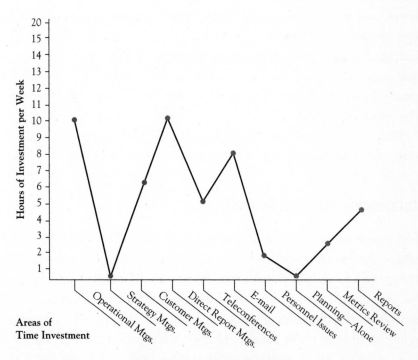

Figure 3.1   Time Gauge

Eliminate	Increase
Reports	Strategy Meetings Planning—Alone
Decrease	**Create**
Operational Meetings E-mail	Strategy-Metrics Updates

Figure 3.2   Time Trade-Off Matrix

while significant time is being invested in operational meetings and meetings with direct reports.

Once the Time Gauge graph has been developed, you can then determine what modifications, if any, need to be made in how you invest your most important resource, time. Changes in time allocation can be catalyzed using the Time Trade-Off Matrix. The Time Trade-Off Matrix examines each area of investment from the Time Gauge and asks you to place the factors with time modifications in the appropriate quadrant. Figure 3.2 represents the Time Trade-Off Matrix for the previous example.

People want more time. What most people really need is more direction and greater discipline in how to use the time they already have.

Influencing Strategy Commitment

Have you experienced a Kodak moment lately? Probably not. The iconic American brand was once synonymous with photography. But, they failed to see the transition from film to digital photography, and became another example of a once-great company that simply didn't anticipate the changing market. At least that's the popular myth that many would have you believe. However, Kodak's fall wasn't due to a lack of vision or poor strategy. The senior leaders did anticipate the move to digital photography and invested early and heavily to create the foundation for a smooth transition. Their failing was their inability to get buy-in from the mid-level managers within Kodak that the strategy was the right one and in the best, long-term interest of the company. Instead, mid-level managers rejected the change in strategic direction to digital and clung to the behaviors that led to their leadership in film. Despite their best efforts, Kodak's senior leaders were unable to influence the rest of the organization to follow their strategy. The inability to influence, not the strategy itself, was at the heart of Kodak's downfall.

Influence is defined as "the power to change or affect someone or something; the power to cause changes without directly forcing them to happen; a person or thing that affects someone or something in an important way."[21] When we attempt to influence, we're trying to connect our goals to other's interests in the hopes that they'll act or behave in a way that we desire. Simply giving someone an order or command to do something without taking the time to connect it to their self-interests may yield results in the short term, but lacks the power of skilled influence in the long term. A study of 7,000 adult workers in the United States found that the average person is spending 40 percent of their time in what's referred to as *non-sales selling*, situations where they are attempting to influence someone but no direct purchase is involved.[22] In the matrix organizational structure employed in many companies, the ability to influence is crucial if one is to gain their share of internal resources and effectively align their priorities with those of other key players.

A survey of 60,000 workers on how well a company's strategy is understood and accepted by employees found that senior leadership is by far the most important factor. The researchers concluded, ". . . top management has a profound impact on how well employees grasp and support strategy—far greater than any other variable we examined and far greater than we'd expected."[23] As Kirk Klasson, former Vice President of Strategy at Novell and current CIO at Cooley LLP said, "No strategy can just be handed down to an organization. Without achieving real understanding and agreement, there will be lots of grinning and backslapping over the strategy but zero change when people get back to their offices."[24]

People tend to accept inner responsibility for their actions when they believe they've had a say in the process and the actions are aligned with some part of their interests. Lacking the ability to contribute input or being unaware of how the task relates to their goals won't generate the necessary level of commitment. The result is a plan that dies a slow death because people weren't afforded the opportunity to provide input into the strategy in the first place. To make matters worse, the strategy has not been translated to what it means for people in their daily work and why they should be following this approach.

During the strategic thinking phase of the strategy development process, people from different functional areas and different levels in the organization should have the opportunity to contribute insights. Having representatives from these different areas share input sends a powerful message to the organization that there is real importance in their work and ideas. Not tapping into the insights of frontline managers, often those closest to the customer and the competition, represents a huge missed opportunity for innovation in the form of anticipating emerging needs. One study found that middle managers account for only 20 percent of the input into an organization's strategy.[25] By allowing managers in different areas and levels to share their insights, senior leaders have a much greater chance for securing buy-in and commitment to the strategy once it's developed. As strategic thinking shouldn't be an annual event, an ongoing channel for insight sharing should be cultivated. This encourages employees to continually mine their daily experiences for ideas to build their base of expertise and pass along to others.

In addition to providing managers with the opportunity to contribute their insights to the strategy, it's equally important to share with everyone *why* the strategy being pursued has been chosen. People don't have to agree with the strategy or the rationale behind the *why*. The important thing is they want to know what the strategy is and why. In essence, they need the *because*, as in "We're doing X, *because* Y." That's it. Research in the social sciences shows that people are much more likely to fulfill a request if you simply give them a reason for doing it. One study had a person standing in line waiting to make copies at a Xerox machine. If the participant asked the person ahead of them, "Excuse me, I have five pages. May I use the Xerox machine?," they were granted permission to go ahead 60 percent of the time. When the end of the request was changed to "May I use the Xerox machine because I'm in a rush?" the permission rate jumped to 94 percent.[26] While the reason, "I'm in a rush," is fairly nebulous, it was prefaced by the magic word: because.

If we don't provide people with the reason behind the strategy, they'll often make one up. In the behavioral sciences, this is referred to as counterfactual thinking. In layman's terms, counterfactual thinking is "second guessing." Second guessing is borne out of people's desire for understanding the reason why something is happening. In the realm of business strategy, people are much less likely to "throw the leader under the bus" if their input was included in the process at some point and they were then given a clear statement of strategy and why it was chosen. To get managers to truly understand and apply strategy in the course of their daily work, you must share with them the *why*.

Increasing Buy-In with Social Proof

In addition to providing people with the reason or *why* behind the strategy, you can also gain a greater level of commitment to the strategy by using social proof. The principle of social proof explains that someone is more likely to behave in a way that is similar to how they see others behave.[27] A common manifestation of this principle in the corporate world can be observed at meetings. If the leaders in an organization are continually 10–15 minutes late for meetings, their people begin to lose regard for the meeting start time as well. Pretty soon, the culture reflects this lack of punctuality and the phrase "fashionably late" becomes the modus operandi.

When it comes to strategy, social proof can be a powerful influence. When employees see their leader fully engaged and committed to a strategy, it demonstrates to them that it isn't another flavor-of-the-month initiative. A leader who takes the time to meet with employees in small groups to discuss strategic direction, translates strategy into concrete actions for those groups, and actively listens to them for new ideas demonstrates a sincere interest in their overall success.

As strategy is built around how one allocates their resources, it's important to be aware of how you as a leader are investing your resources, especially time. Your investment behaviors will be a strong driver of how others invest their resources. Declaring a tailored solutions-oriented strategy built around customer intimacy and then lacking the discipline to not check e-mail during internal meetings in which customers are being discussed reeks of hypocrisy. Driving strategies to forge product leadership positions in the market and then cutting the budget for professional development as soon as there's a dip in revenues also snuffs out the power of social proof. A leader's words can move people to action, but a leader's actions can move people to commitment.

One of the challenges leaders face in getting their people to commit to a strategy is in the nature of strategy itself. A sound strategy declares trade-offs, resulting in change and new direction. A recent study on creativity showed that people automatically assume that a novel idea is not reliable or practical and likely contains errors.[28] New strategies are instantly working against a tide of doubt, not to mention people's reluctance to change. Therefore, another application of the principle of social proof is to provide people with evidence that the chosen strategy provides the best course of action. Since people look to others for guidance on how they should act, giving employees examples or testimonials can be a powerful way to influence. Finding examples of other brands within the company or other companies outside the industry that were in a similar situation and succeeded with a similar strategic approach can be affirming. If your team finds itself entering a recently deregulated market as a challenger to several established incumbents, it may be helpful to explain how a company like Southwest Airlines found itself in a similar situation and made unique trade-offs to forge a niche position that led to decades of profitable growth.

The use of testimonials has a long track record of success influencing behavior. While they can range from the ridiculous late-night infomercials to the weighty support of a presidential candidate, a testimonial represents a written or spoken statement of support for a person, product, or service. Testimonials can assist in the effective implementation of strategy through the ongoing strategy dialogue process. As you have periodic strategy conversations with colleagues, be sure to record success stories and anecdotes that reflect the positive impact the strategy is having in driving customer value. A powerful technique is to video record these success stories and best practices in implementing strategy and share them internally in town-hall meetings, presentations, and intranets. Since one of the biggest obstacles to effective strategy execution is overcoming silos between different functional areas or geographic locations, the opportunity for colleagues to see and hear directly from their counterparts, either live or through video, can give them further social proof that the strategy is worthy of their commitment.

Another method for employing the power of social proof is to share pictures of success from other divisions, brands, areas, or managers that have fully adopted a strategy. Simply compare and contrast the strategies and results of two groups. If one group, location, or branch, has committed to the strategy and generated improved results while another group wedded to the old approach hasn't, graphically show these different approaches and their corresponding results in a memorable way. For instance, showing a picture of a rugged off-road jeep climbing over boulders with "7 percent gain in operating margins" as the caption can illustrate the success of a team that has followed the new strategic direction despite lots of obstacles and achieved success. Then, contrast it with picture of a 1970s station wagon driving by a 25 miles per hour speed limit sign with the caption "0 percent improvement in operating margins" to represent the teams not yet committed to the new strategy. Research shows that people generally understand things better when they see those things in comparison to something else, instead of in isolation.[29] Contrast breeds clarity.

In seeking to influence others to commit to a strategy, a leader can focus energy solely on those they're attempting to persuade. However, this overlooks an important persuasive tool, the environment. Sometimes, simply changing physical things in people's environment can alter their mindset or behavior. One study showed that people attending a movie right after lunch were influenced to eat different amounts of popcorn based purely on the size of the bucket they were given. Despite just having finished lunch, the researchers found that people who were given large buckets of popcorn ate 53 percent more than those with smaller buckets.[30] Amazon.com CEO Jeff Bezos is reported to occasionally leave one chair open at a conference table to represent their customer.[31] By changing an element in their physical environment—in this case adding an empty chair—Bezos has created another influence to demonstrate to employees the importance of the customer in the development and execution of their strategies. He says, "We innovate by starting with the customer and working backwards. That becomes the touchstone for how we invent."[32] Concepts change thinking and tools change behavior. Finding ways to create physical reminders in your manager's environment on the important elements of the strategy is crucial to sustaining momentum throughout the year.

As you hone your strategy and communicate it with others in the organization, it's important to bring it to a personal level. One of the reasons strategic planning has become a mind-numbingly, ambiguous exercise is because it's not translated to the individual level. Managers work to feed a PowerPoint deck with information and data that they themselves won't use after the dog-and-pony show presentation is concluded. A sociology study on the donation behaviors of individuals sheds some light on why this might occur. The study showed that people are more willing to donate money to help a single starving African child than to help many starving children. Interestingly, the researcher also found that contributions dropped dramatically when the individual child's picture was accompanied by a statistical summary of the large number of needy children like her in other countries.[33] Similarly, when we see a specific, individualized issue, we are more likely to respond to it. When we're faced with a general blob of information, we tend to tune it out. The lesson for leaders: Tailor the meaning of the strategy to your audience and how it relates specifically to them and what they're doing on a daily basis. As Mother Teresa said, "If I look at the mass, I will never act. If I look at the one, I will."

Strategic Behavior

It turns out that all influence geniuses focus on behaviors. . . . They don't develop an influence strategy until they've carefully identified the specific behaviors they want to change. They start by asking: In order to improve our existing situation, what must people actually do?
　—Authors of *Influencer: The Power to Change Anything*

The ability to influence others to commit to goals and strategies over the long-term doesn't come from a one-time motivational speech or a colorful banner at the national sales meeting. As evidenced by the research presented in the preceding section, the success of influence is determined by one's ability to shape other's behaviors. A behavior is defined in its simplest form as an observable activity.[34] Behaviors fundamentally change one's relationship to their environment, sometimes in a positive way and sometimes in a negative way. Beginning in childhood, as parents coerce their children to eat more vegetables, behaviors are continually being shaped.

At its foundation, influencing another's behavior comes down to addressing two questions for them: 1) Is it worth it? 2) Can I do it?[35] The first question addresses the benefit and the second question addresses the belief. People first and foremost want to know why they should do something, and need to have the belief that it can be done. Instilling the belief that it can be done is a matter of showing them the path or technique to do it. Advising someone to quit smoking without arming them with proven techniques for doing so will result in zero behavioral change. A teacher admonishing a student to *pay attention*, which is vague and non-directional, has a much greater opportunity for positively influencing the student's behavior by saying instead, "Eyes forward, feet on the floor, and hand up to speak." Telling a group of managers to be innovative and think out of the box is use-less. Instead, sharing with them how to use the Value Mining Matrix (discussed in Discipline #1) to assess current and potential customers and their existing and emerging jobs to be done, while providing an example for each helps them *behave* out of the box. Whether it's at home, school, or work, behavioral direction needs to be specific, con-crete, and observable.[36]

When developing new behaviors for a group to effectively create and implement strategies, remember the power of games. Games are an effective way to keep people fully engaged in an activity. A game typically involves goals, rules, challenges, and interaction. Professor Mihaly Csikszentmihalyi, a leader in the field of positive psychology, showed that activities involving game criteria such as goals, rules, and clear feedback can create *flow*: the state in which people become so engrossed with an activity that it creates an optimal state of inner experience.[37] As you design new behaviors to implement strategies, attempt to include built-in opportunities to loop in goals, guidelines, challenges, and frequent feedback.

While sales teams are the group most commonly receiving goals (sales numbers) and frequent feedback (sales results), they generally lack sufficient guidelines for winning their game. The sales arena in particular suffers from the "activity = achievement" mentality. For many years, in industries such as pharmaceuticals and consumer pack-aged goods, having the greatest reach and frequency numbers were the key to success. That isn't always the case today. Great sales leaders realize it's no longer enough to know the competitor's product specifi-cations inside and out. Today, top sales managers also understand their competitor's overall strategic approach to the market and help their sales reps develop behaviors to attack those strategies.

One such behavior of advanced sales representatives is to cre-ate a Competitive Advantage Profile for their top five accounts. Strategic sales reps can use the Competitive Advantage Profile to break down the core competencies, capabilities, and business model of the competition and then target weaknesses in the competitor's strategic approach to bring unique value to those accounts. Other internal groups such as human resources, information technology, and research and development tend to be lighter on the goal and frequent feedback criteria. The important thing to understand is that the behaviors you develop should contain the game and flow criteria to build a greater sense of inner fulfillment and drive within your team members.

In my prior book, *Deep Dive: The Proven Method for Building Strategy*, I introduced the premise: *New growth comes from new thinking.*[38] A strategic leader understands that their role is to not only to stimulate this new thinking for their group, it's also to ensure it's accompanied by the appropriate behaviors to generate new growth. We can capture this notion in an advanced premise: **New thinking inspires new behavior, leading to new results**. The term *inspire* is defined as "to exert an animating, enlivening, or exalting influence," and as the epigraph to this section states, ". . . all influence geniuses focus on behaviors."[39]

To prepare your business for new results, ask the following 12 questions:

1. What are the three to five key behaviors that have driven my success in the past?

2. What are three to five behaviors that my colleagues have used to drive their success?

3. What are three to five behaviors that my competitors have used to drive their success?

4. What are three to five behaviors that have held my business back from reaching its full potential?

5. Based on my business's situation and strengths, and the context and opportunities of the market, which behaviors are most likely to create success?

6. What resource investments in time, talent, and budget will be required to make these behaviors happen on a daily basis?

7. Will the current corporate culture support or suppress these new behaviors?

8. What is the most relevant reason *why* people should adopt these behaviors?

9. How can I most effectively communicate the reason *why* people should adopt these behaviors?

10. What specific, concrete, and observable directions can I provide to embed these behaviors in our team?

11. How will I measure the level of commitment to these new behaviors?

12. Which metrics will best track these behavior's effects on the business?

Practicing Strategic Thinking

Once you've identified the behaviors that will have the most impact on the success of your business, it's important to give your people an opportunity to practice them on a regular basis. In professional sports such as Major League Baseball, multi-million dollar professional athletes spend six to eight weeks in spring training before each season practicing the fundamentals: throwing, catching, hitting, fielding, bunting, and so on. In fact, professional athletes spend about 90 percent of their time practicing and only about 10 percent performing in their competition.[40] In the business arena, those numbers are reversed, with the reality being that many executives are not even close to practicing or training 10 percent of their time. Research with more than 3,000 human resource executives showed that senior executives receive the least amount of training, and 41 percent receive no training and development at all.[41] It's ironic that as a leader assumes more responsibility and makes decisions that have a much greater impact on the overall business, they're given less practice and training.

Practice is defined as "to perform or work at repeatedly so as to become proficient; to train by repeated exercises."[42] While we most often see the applicability of practice to sports, music, and hobbies, the reality is that practice is also integral to success in intellectual pursuits. United States Supreme Court Chief Justice John Roberts Jr.'s intellectual rigor and success in his field are due in large part to his willingness and discipline to practice. Writer Roger Parloff describes Chief Justice Robert's practice habits:

When Roberts was preparing an oral argument, he would write down—usually longhand, using a pen and a legal pad—hundreds of questions that he might conceivably be asked. He'd ponder and refine the answers in his mind. Then he'd write the questions on flash cards, shuffle them, and test himself, so he'd be prepared to answer any question in any order.[43]

Chief Justice Roberts explained this approach with oral advocates in a speech: "The advocate . . . must meticulously prepare, analyze, and rehearse answers to hundreds of questions, questions that in all likelihood will actually never be asked by the court."[44]

Renowned surgeon and professor Atul Gawande echoes the value of practice when he came to the following realization: "I'd paid to have a kid just out of college look at my tennis serve. So why did I find it inconceivable to pay someone to come into my operating room and coach me on my surgical technique?"[45] Dr. Gawande's insight demonstrates that high performers in intellectual fields generally don't even consider practicing because of the very fact that *they are high performers in an intellectual field*. This is often the case with senior leaders in organizations. When conducting strategic-thinking workshops with director-level managers, one of the common themes that emerges is, "Our senior leaders need this training as well." Understanding that practicing the behaviors critical to one's role is important at any level of the organization opens up the potential for dramatic organizational improvement. The next step is determining how to practice those behaviors.

As children, we're taught that practice is the key to improving our skill, whether it be playing the piano, hitting a baseball, or mastering multiplication tables. What we learn as adults is that all practice is not equally valuable. Spend 10 minutes at the driving range and it's quickly evident that hitting ball after ball with no practice goals, feedback mechanism, or deliberate adjustments might be enjoyable, but it won't make you better at golf. It would seem to reason that in a highly educated profession such as medicine, doctors would naturally get better over time. However, research shows that in many cases they don't. In fact, mammographers generally become less accurate over time.[46] *Influencer* author Kerry Patterson writes, "A 20-year-veteran brain surgeon is not likely to be any more skilled than a 5-year rookie by virtue of time on the job. Any difference between the two would have nothing to do with experience and everything to do with deliberate practice. . . . It's the *skill* of practice that makes perfect."[47] Therefore, a closer look at the science behind practice and skill building can give us a clearer path to developing effective behaviors.

A behavior is an observable activity. An activity is made up of thoughts and movements. These thoughts and movements are the result of precisely timed electrical signals moving through a circuit of nerve fibers or chain of neurons. The nerve fibers are wrapped with an electrical insulator called myelin. Myelin insulates these nerve fibers like rubber insulation wraps a wire, increasing the speed, strength, and accuracy of the signal.[48] The more we practice a certain activity, the greater the number of myelin layers that wrap around that circuit. More myelin insulation allows for quicker, more precise thoughts and movements, leading to a higher level of skill in that behavior. UCLA neurologist Dr. George Bartzokis summarizes by saying, "All skills, language, all music, all movements are made up of living circuits and all circuits grow according to certain rules. . . . What do good athletes do when they train? They send precise impulses along wires that give the signal to myelinate that wire."[49]

In order to effectively develop a new behavior, it's helpful to break the behavior down into its component pieces, practice those pieces individually, and then practice those pieces together. When practicing the individual pieces, it's more effective to do so slowly, allowing for mistakes and then correcting those mistakes as you go. If you've ever attempted to improve your golf swing, you know that you wouldn't try and change the entire swing at once. A golf instructor assisting you would first break your swing down to look at its components: stance, grip, shoulder and head position, club take-away, backswing, form at the top, downswing, arm position, hand position at contact, follow through, and finishing position. Once that analysis has been completed, you'd then pick one of those pieces and work on building what's often referred to as *muscle memory*, or more precisely, greater myelination around the appropriate nerve bundle. Each time you struggle with an individual piece of the behavior, then perform it optimally, you're slowly building more myelin around the circuit and increasing the skill level.

Let's use the strategic thinking behavior of resource allocation as an example. Instructing someone to "allocate their resources more effectively" would probably be met with a look of bewilderment. There are a number of thoughts and activities that go into the behavior of effective resource allocation, so it's helpful to break the behavior down into its components. First, we should identify the individual circuits in the behavior of resource allocation. A sample might include the following:

- List of activities where time is invested
- Analysis of how much time is invested in each activity
- Creation of a graph to visually depict time investment per activity
- Use of a Time Trade-Off Matrix to determine which activities to eliminate investment of time, decrease investment of time, increase investment of time, and create new investment areas
- Recreation of graph with a new line depicting future allocation of the resource time
- List of action steps required to make the time trade-offs identified

A major reason managers don't become more strategic over time is because they only perform the related tasks once a year during the annual planning process. In order to build up greater layers of myelin around our strategic-thinking circuits, we need to practice thinking strategically on a regular basis. A skill deteriorates if the primary circuits comprising the activities in a particular behavior are not used for 30 days.[50] If you're not dedicating time at least monthly to questions and frameworks to think strategically about the business, then you will not be strategic.

Leaders have the opportunity to not only practice key behaviors themselves, but also to continually hone and develop their people's skills during their daily interactions. Opportunities for shaping how your managers practice include one-to-one conversations, customer visits, and staff meetings. Monthly strategy dialogues and workshops can be highly formative experiences that raise everyone's performance. As these situations arise, there are three practice principles that can guide your instruction.

Practice Principle #1: Begin with the Goal

If you've ever coached your young child's sports team, you understand the challenges of balancing the fun factor with actually teaching them skills to improve. With all that energy on the field or court, it's easy to get caught up in a cycle of rapid-fire drills or chaotic scrimmages just to keep things moving along. But, no matter the age group, each practice needs to have at least one goal to work toward. The goal is what you are trying to achieve during that practice. Goals can include faster footwork, better defense, improved fielding, and so on. Once the goals have been identified prior to the practice, the activities that build toward the goals can be chosen.

The same holds true for managers. When you look at each manager and the responsibilities they have, what goals will help them improve their key behaviors? In other words, what should they be trying to achieve when practicing that behavior? Is the goal to improve their understanding of a competitor's strategic approach to the market? Is the goal developing medical-expert relationships to secure a greater number of clinical trials at a key academic hospital? Is the goal influencing without authority in order to align priorities across different functional areas in the organization? Determining the goal of the practice is step one.

Practice Principle #2: Break the Whole into Pieces

As discussed earlier, new behaviors are most effectively mastered when they are broken into their individual components. Once in the individual components, each piece can then be practiced slowly and repeatedly until that circuit has built up more bandwidth. An Olympic diver masters each chunk of the dive and then puts them together during the competition so that they flow together automatically. By mastering each piece separately and adding myelin to the corresponding neural circuit, the diver can begin a dive by activating the first skill circuit, which leads into the next, and the next.

Once a manager has a goal to practice, the next step is to break that behavior into its individual pieces. The earlier example on the behavior of resource allocation illustrates the steps that one can take to break it down into its individual components and then work to master each step. Mastery is then demonstrated when the manager can seamlessly weave together the individual elements of the behavior into its whole. To assist in the process, use a visual flow chart to plot the separate pieces and show the manager how each part fits into the sum of the behavior.

Practice Principle #3: Correct with a Solution

The great teachers and coaches are skilled in correcting their students or athletes and then providing them with an immediate opportunity to practice the activity again to improve on it. In using the case-study method of teaching business, the instructor enters into dialogues with students. These dialogues are peppered with questions and suggestions to move the student's thinking forward to identify the core problem in the case, devise a minimum of three to five alternatives to solve it and select one alternative as their recommendation. A sample dialogue might go something like this:

Professor: Why isn't the company profitable?

Student: They need to expand internationally.

Professor: That's a potential alternative. What is the reason why the company is not profitable?

Student: Oh, there's new competition.

Professor: And how is the new competitor positioned in the market?

Student: They're the low-cost leader.

Professor: So, how has that affected the company?

Student: They've lowered their prices to match this new competitor. Because they've lowered their prices, they no longer command high margins. And that's why they're not profitable.

While it would have been easier and faster for the professor to interject much earlier in the conversation, it wouldn't have provided the student with the practice necessary to get to the proper conclusion. The use of correction ("That's a potential alternative. What is the reason . . .") and the series of developing questions enabled the following formula to take place:

Practice ➡ Correction ➡ Repractice

Correction differs from criticism. Criticism takes place when you tell someone they did something wrong, often using a negative. In the case of a basketball player, a criticism might be, "Stop lunging on defense!" A correction in this case could be the following, "Angle your shoulders to the side and shuffle your feet." The correction provides specific, concrete direction on how to improve and then gives the person a chance to enact the feedback immediately.

Legendary college basketball coach John Wooden, who led the UCLA men's basketball team to 10 national championships, was studied in the 1970s to better understand his highly successful practice habits. The researchers recorded and coded more than 2,000 discrete acts of teaching during his practices. Of these, only 6.9 percent were compliments and 6.6 percent were expressions of displeasure. The vast majority, 75 percent, were pure information: simple directions on how to play basketball.[51] Coach Wooden didn't waste time with long, monologue critiques of his players. He told them what he wanted them to do and had them immediately do it. One of his former players described the process: "It was the information I received, during the correction, that I needed most. Having received it, I could then make the adjustments and changes needed. It was the information that promoted change."[52] Coach Wooden didn't waste time with evaluations ("No, that's not right. What are you thinking!"). He provided clear, concise, and informative solutions. How much time each day do you spend on trite praise or long-winded criticism? When you observe your managers' behaviors, are you offering informative solutions to improve?

Developing Strategy Habits

The result of practicing a behavior over and over can be the formation of a habit. A habit is defined as, "a behavior pattern acquired by frequent repetition or physiologic exposure that shows itself in regularity or increased facility of performance; an acquired mode of behavior that has become nearly or completely involuntary."[53] Depending on the behavior, the habit can be positive (e.g., exercising each morning) or negative (e.g., uncontrolled gambling). The goal is to foster positive habits and transform negative habits into positive ones. As anyone who has tried to break a bad habit knows, it's much easier said than done.

Researchers at the Massachusetts Institute of Technology have shed light onto the science behind habits.[54] A habit consists of the following three components:

1. Cue (trigger)
2. Routine (behavior)
3. Reward (result)

This neurological loop is at the core of our habits, both good and bad. The cue for a positive habit like exercising in the morning might be your dog waking you up at 6 a.m. with a lick on the hand. The routine would be jogging along the lake, and the reward is an ice-cold, chocolate protein shake. The cue for a detrimental habit like uncontrolled gambling might be boredom. The routine would be going to a

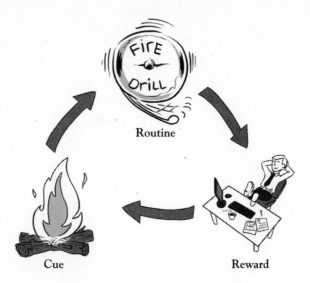

Routine

Cue

Reward

Figure 3.3   Fire Drill Habit

tavern and playing video poker, and the reward is the excitement (or lack of boredom) that comes from winning or from the near misses of almost winning. All habits follow this route of cue, routine, and reward. We can use this habit model to improve our approach to strategy by creating good habits and eliminating negative ones.

One of the most debilitating habits in business is the fire drill. The fire drill is when people stop purposeful work that is guided by their strategic plan and rush to take care of something urgent that just popped up. If the urgent issue is also important, then naturally it should be taken care of. Unfortunately, many fires are urgent but unimportant. Yet, they still get lots of attention, which wastes valuable time, people, and budget. The fire drill habit is represented in Figure 3.3.

The key to eliminating a bad habit is to replace the routine, or behavior, with a more positive or productive one. By keeping the same cue and same reward, this shift in the routine can transform the bad habit into a good one.[55] In the fire drill example, it's to be expected that fires will continue to pop up during the course of business, even if some can be prevented by understanding the root causes in their systems. When the cue or fire triggers the habit, we need to replace the current routine—a flurry of unplanned activity—with a new one.

Figure 3.4   Modifying the Fire Drill Habit

A phrase as simple as "Let's think about that," can fill the routine. This phrase reminds people not to just react to the fire, but to consider it relative to the other planned initiatives currently being worked on. Do we really need to attend to this? Does this fall within our responsibilities? Who can handle this more efficiently? How did this fire start in the first place? Figure 3.4 shows the new habit.

We can also proactively build positive business habits using this same technique. Let's say you have a situation where your frontline managers are tactical, but not strategic. So, you'd like to develop their strategic thinking skills into a behavior that becomes a positive habit. The cue would be a business challenge, such as new competitor activities within their market. The current routine consists of managers working in the weeds of the business and only offering up tactics. The result is revenue, but only enough to survive (Figure 3.5).

To modify this habit, you'd replace the current tactical routine with development of strategic thinking skills using the three basic disciplines to: identify the insight (acumen), focus resources through trade-offs (allocation), and effectively execute the strategy (action).

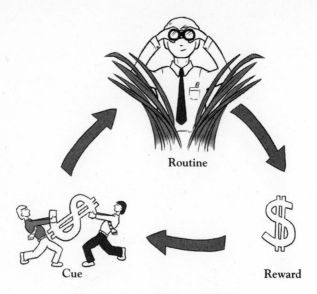

Figure 3.5   Tactical Habit

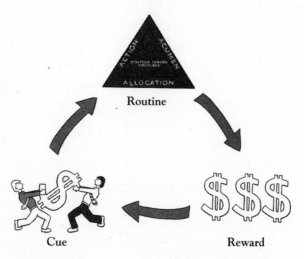

Figure 3.6   Strategic Thinking Habit

The result is outperforming the competitor and increasing profits significantly for the organization. We can represent this new habit using the cue-routine-reward framework in Figure 3.6.

A nearly universal business habit that can be enhanced in many cases is strategic planning. For many organizations, the cue for this

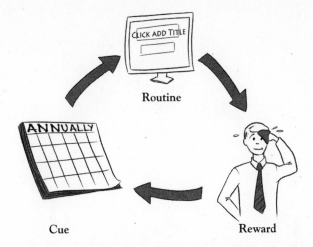

Figure 3.7   Annual Strategic Planning Habit

behavior is the calendar. As the calendar hits October or November, it triggers the routine or behavior of strategic planning. The more seasoned, or cynical, manager might describe the routine as filling out a bunch of templates that create a huge PowerPoint slide deck. The reward is a sense of accomplishment, or relief, and a tangible plan. The habit is represented in Figure 3.7.

However, with just a few adjustments, the strategic planning process can be made much more productive and relevant. The first adjustment keeps the same cue (calendar), but instead of an annual trigger, it becomes monthly. The monthly cue triggers a new routine consisting of a half-day strategic thinking session to accumulate new insights and review existing goals, objectives, strategies, tactics, and metrics, and make the appropriate modifications. The result is a real-time strategic action plan that is highly relevant, drives people's daily activities, and instills greater confidence in the strategic direction. The new habit is illustrated in Figure 3.8.

The following 10 questions can improve your team's strategy habits:

1. What is the top strategy habit you'd like to change for the group?
2. What is the cue, routine, and reward?

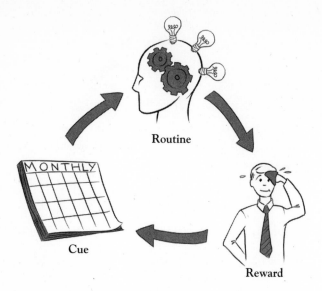

Figure 3.8   Monthly Strategy Assessment Habit

3. What new routine could you substitute to transform the habit?

4. What is the top strategy habit you'd like to change for yourself?

5. What is the cue, routine, and reward?

6. What new routine could you substitute to transform the habit?

7. What new habit would you like to create?

8. What would comprise the cue, routine, and reward?

9. What resource allocation changes would need to occur to create this habit?

10. What cultural or organizational changes would need to occur to ensure the habit lasts?

Strategy Conversations

For some organizations, strategic planning is similar to the mating ritual of penguins. Emperor penguins waddle up to 75 miles once a year to mate for a few minutes and then the female immediately leaves. That's not much different than managers making the annual pilgrimage to the off-site strategic-planning meeting for two days and then returning to the office to get back to their "real" work. Strategy should not be an event. Strategy should be an ongoing conversation.

One of the keys to maximizing your strategic leadership potential is to facilitate effective strategy conversations. A strategy conversation is a systematic method of encouraging the exchange of ideas, beliefs, and opinions on the key strategic elements of a business. The term *conversation* stems from the Latin *con versare*, which means "turning together." In a strategy conversation, the participants mentally move with one another from point to point. Three characteristics promote healthy strategy conversations:

1. **Candor**: The willingness to express honest ideas and opinions
2. **Suspension**: The discipline to actively listen without judging
3. **Openness**: The ability to thrive in a situation where the outcome is unknown

The participants' ability to embrace these criteria can encourage new and different perspectives that can generate breakthrough strategy. The leader's actions play a large role in determining the effectiveness of a team's strategy conversations. If a leader is quick to criticize opinions and ideas instead of thoughtfully inquiring about them, managers will determine it's not in their political best interest to show candor. If people are not able to suspend judgment and their body language includes eye rolls and stares of disapproval, then the conversation will quickly shut down. It takes a strong manager to mentally wade into conversations filled with ambiguous gray areas, especially when he or she is not fully armed with all the answers. Yet, these are the rare leaders that fully tap into the intellectual capital and insights residing in their managers' minds.

A conversation is comprised of two types of exchanges: dialogue and discussion. While the two terms are often used interchangeably, it's important to note the distinction as you facilitate strategy conversations amongst your team. New strategy conversations begin with dialogue. A dialogue is an exchange of ideas or opinions on a particular issue. Think about your organization's strategic planning process. Is it grounded in this open exchange of ideas and opinions? Or do new ideas need to survive a series of didactic monologues and a gauntlet of leadership critiques?

The term *dialogue* comes from the Greek roots *dia-* and *-logue* signifying "a flow of meaning through words."[56] A strategy dialogue facilitates the exchange of insights and understanding between two or more people on the important issues of the business. The key is to have these strategy dialogues on a regular basis, not just once a year at the strategic planning meeting or off-site retreat. As author Ram Charan notes, "Dialogue can lead to new ideas and speed as a competitive advantage. It is the single-most important factor underlying the productivity and growth of the knowledge worker."[57]

Once the group has exhausted the topics of strategic relevance through dialogue, the facilitator directs the group to begin discussion. Through discussion, the group breaks down the insights generated in the exploratory dialogue phase, and harnesses them to develop solutions that move things forward. What emerges from the discussion are the actionable strategies, accountability, and implementation that bring the conversation its end result. This is where focus becomes clear, trade-offs are weighed, and decisions are made.

Unfortunately, many strategy development teams *begin* with a discussion mindset. Instead of starting with a preliminary dialogue rooted in an open exchange of ideas that explore uncertainties and unknowns, people immediately propose solutions in the form of tactics. This undermines the innovative, assumption-challenging, and exploratory nature of dialogue, which is an essential element of an effective strategy conversation. Groups that jump right into strategic *planning* without first engaging in strategic *thinking* are also likely to overlook new ideas, opportunities, and tactics. The result is the same tired plan that causes an organization to stagnate and lose interest in the strategy development process altogether.

Strategy conversations should occur frequently, in both formal and informal settings. They are not a replacement for the strategy development process; they are simply a technique to engage in throughout the year to complement the strategy development process and enhance its effectiveness and output. Just as an extension to the handle of a wrench will yield greater leverage to turn a difficult bolt, a strategy conversation serves to enhance the effectiveness and efficiency of the strategy development process. There are three steps to introducing strategy conversations to your management team.

1. **Educate on the strategy conversation technique.** Provide managers with a primer on the difference between dialogue and discussion, as well as notes outlining the questions, tools, and techniques for leading strategy conversations amongst their teams. Ensure people begin with a dialogue—an open exchange of ideas and opinions—and do not jump right to tactical solutions.

2. **Record insights from strategy conversations.** Managers should keep a log of their insights from both formal and informal strategy conversations in order to build their body of expertise. During every encounter, strategic leaders should continually ask themselves, "What is my insight, knowledge, or take-away from this exchange?"

3. **Engage people from other areas and levels.** Seek out people from different functional areas and levels of the organization to engage them in strategy dialogue to stimulate new thinking. A fresh perspective from a different vantage point can often open up new channels of thought. London Business School professor Don Sull writes:

Strategy discussions should not be concentrated at the top; they must take place at every level of the organization. Strategy will remain stranded in the executive suites unless teams throughout the organization can effectively translate broad corporate objectives into concrete action.[58]

The conclusion of a strategy conversation should be marked with a form of commitment. The commitment is determined by whether the conversation was in the exploratory dialogue phase or in the solution-seeking discussion phase. The commitment may be as simple as scheduling a follow-up conversation or as intensive as creating a war room to compile intelligence on the launch of a new competitor. The important thing is to leave the conversation with some course of action in place. Upon the conclusion of a strategy conversation, you'll also want to record the key insights, knowledge, or takeaways from the exchange to continue to build your base of expertise. As J. Bruce Harreld, former leader of the IBM Strategy Unit wrote, "The essence of strategy is disciplined, fact-based conversations."[59]

The Power of Story

Try this quick exercise: Write down from memory as much of last year's strategic plan as you can recall off the top of your head. Then on a second sheet of paper, write down as much of the story "Goldilocks and the Three Bears" as you can remember. Despite the fact that the strategic plan was written within the past 12 months and it's probably been decades since you've read "The Three Bears" (unless you have small children), it's likely that you recalled more of the Goldilocks's story than the strategic plan. Why? As cognitive psychologists have established from years of research, stories are more memorable than bulleted lists, which tend to make up much of today's strategic-planning PowerPoint decks.

A story is an account of events or experiences, either true or fictitious, in narrative form. Research shows that because a story's elements are packaged into a single, linear narrative comprised of the setting, characters, relationships, sequences of events, conflict, and resolution, it is easier for our minds to retain the information a story conveys.[60] Lists of bullet points that lack narrative flow suffer from the *recency effect* and the *primacy effect*, meaning that people are more likely to remember the first and last items on the list, but not much in between.

Researcher Michael Carriger conducted a study to compare how well employees retained information about corporate strategy presented in bulleted versus narrative format. One set of employees was presented with a PowerPoint version of the corporate strategy. Four months following the presentation, 29 percent of employees identified the strategy as one of differentiation, 58 percent identified it as focusing on customer intimacy, and 13 percent on cost leadership.[61] The average confidence rating employees gave their response was only 2.9 on a scale of 5. So, not only was there poor recall of the strategy, but employees knew that they were uncertain of it. Carriger concluded, "Intriguingly, a narrative presentation, in the form of a 'springboard story' would appear to be a more effective means to lead employees to understand what strategy is than a bullet-point list of facts and figures reminiscent of the typical PowerPoint presentation."[62]

Unlike bullet points strung together across slides, a story forces the creator to demonstrate their mastery of the material by showing the reader the all-important connections and relationships between the key components. A story enables the reader to visualize the setting, see the characters, identify the challenges or conflicts preventing their success, establish how the journey forward unfolds, and describe the final resolution. Much of Amazon.com's success in anticipating customer needs and providing comprehensive solutions to large-scale challenges (e.g., same-day delivery, cloud services, video streaming, etc.) can be attributed to the high-level of strategic thinking that takes place throughout the organization in the form of narrative. CEO Jeff Bezos has his team prepare six-page narratives, which are read in silence at the beginning of meetings before being discussed. Describing the benefits of creating these narratives, Bezos says, "Full sentences are harder to write. They have verbs. The paragraphs have topic sentences. There is no way to write a six-page, narratively structured memo and not have clear thinking."[63]

The nature of story is a fitting way to present strategy for several reasons. Strategy involves trade-offs, which inherently mean that someone is taking a risk. Good stories can effectively convey the element of drama, in this case risk, because they arouse emotions. Too often, strategy is presented in a dry, lifeless, numbers-based approach that inspires no one. Presenting strategy in a narrative form forces us to examine what exactly we can become passionate about within our approach to achieving our goals. If we can't find that excitement or emotion in our strategy, then we haven't made the requisite trade-offs, or we are simply going through the motions. In either case, failure is likely.

Stories have protagonists, in some cases heroes that win the day. They also contain antagonists, who try to prevent protagonists from reaching their goals. While the purpose of strategy is to configure resources to create superior value for customers, painting your team as the hero, and a key competitor or market constraint as the villain, may in some cases spark employees' competitive fires if they aren't currently lit. Several years ago, Apple ran an advertising campaign for their Macintosh computer line that presented Microsoft's product as the geeky villain. More recently, Samsung's ads feature their mobile phone as the new hero, positioning Apple's iPhone—especially the Siri feature—as the outdated villain. Narrative can give your team a rallying cry and inspire their efforts to outperform a marketplace villain.

Great stories also build tension between the current state and the great unknown. As we watch movies or read books, we're continually asking ourselves questions like, "Will they get out alive?," "Can the ship survive the storm?," and "Is she the real murderer?" Effective stories take us into the unknown, let us wallow in uncertainty, and then show us some form of resolution. Creating, communicating, and executing strategy also involves tension (*What trade-offs must be made?*), anxiety about the unknown (*What will our strategy be?*), and uncertain outcomes (*Will we succeed or fail?*). The story format can convey the tone of your specific situation, ranging from the confidence of a market leader to the aggressive desperation of a challenger with only one product and six months of cash left.

Finally, stories enable you to create a lasting visual impression. "Jack and the Beanstalk," "Rudolph the Red-Nosed Reindeer," "Snow White and the Seven Dwarfs." Each story creates a series of pictures in our mind, which we can piece together, much like Walt Disney did in creating his animated cartoons. If we intend to move people to action, to follow our lead, then using stories filled with image-generating words can be an effective tool. Researchers examined the key speeches and inaugural addresses of U.S. presidents to determine the relationship between their speaking styles and the level of inspiration felt by their audiences. The study showed that the greater the number of image-based words used in the speech, the higher the president's leadership rating. The author presenting the research concluded, "Presidents who verbally painted a picture of their vision were best at persuading others to follow them."[64] Employing stories that paint mental pictures give leaders a better chance of persuading their teams to commit to strategic direction.

Creating a Strategy Story

The Strategy Story is a technique that describes your current situation and the strategic approach you're going to take to lead your team to success. Below are the key elements of an effective Strategy Story:

Situation: A description of the current state of your business, including insights on the market, competitive position, goals, etc.

Players: The primary internal and external characters involved in the success or failure of the business. Players can be people, departments, companies, entities, and so on. Since there are potentially hundreds of players, focus on the handful that you believe are the true drivers of success or potential causes of failure.

Challenge: The primary obstacle you face leading your business at this time. Consider traditional competitors, intangible forms of competition (e.g., status quo, low morale, etc.), and internal issues (e.g., turf battles, share of mind, resource allocation, etc.). The main challenge should be singular in nature. It's the one challenge with the most potential to affect your business—in a positive way if it is solved and in a negative way if it is not.

Issues: These are the critical elements underlying the main challenge. They add layers of complexity to the situation and can include smaller challenges that could get in the way of arriving at a resolution.

Options: The three to five mutually exclusive alternatives available for addressing the challenge. Consider the pros and cons of each option to examine the full range of things you can do to solve the main problem facing the business.

Resolution: The strategy for overcoming the primary challenge that will also lead to the achievement of the goal identified in the situation. The resolution should be one of the three to five options generated earlier in the narrative.

Actions: Clear, specific, and realistic steps to take to implement the resolution, including the who, what, and when.

Theme: Great stories have a central theme or premise (e.g., good versus evil, favorite versus underdog) represented by a metaphor, symbol or image (e.g., a mountain peak for achievement, an all-terrain vehicle to take a new or different path to success). Consider the theme and a metaphor, symbol, or image that represents the essence of the story.

The following is an example of a Strategy Story, with the specific section of the story called out in brackets:

[*Situation*] *It's been a tough year. Sales are growing incrementally, but our margins have been shrinking dramatically. We're nine months into the launch of our new product and we're behind forecast. It's a great product, but as you all know we're up against Gargantuan, the 800-pound gorilla in the market. Our primary goal this year is to grow sales and achieve 25 percent profit margins. If we don't hit this, we may not be around in two years.*

[*Players*] *As head of marketing, Marsha has created a strong brand platform for our new product. Her experience in consumer marketing and digital promotion has created a campaign with a lot of buzz in this B-to-B space. With the advantages and benefits the product has, it seems that going in with a premium price made sense. While we have some solid mid-sized clients on board like Everon and Myott, we haven't been able to gain traction with the larger potential customers like Armenium and Staylance. As VP of sales, Steve has been working tirelessly with his team to grow revenues by offering price discounts to get our foot in the door. Gargantuan has been in the market for five years and they've relied on a "good enough" product at a mid-level price point. The other mom-and-pop competitors have little bits and pieces of the market in their local niches.*

[Challenge] *It seems to me that the biggest challenge we face is a disconnect between our value proposition and real-world pricing strategies. We have a product with greater benefits and value to customers than Gargantuan's offering, but it comes at a higher price. So we're offering a premium product, but then we're discounting the heck out of it when we're face-to-face with customers in order to get our foot in the door and make a sale. It seems that Marsha and Steve are working off of completely different plans. Something has to give.*

[Options] *Let's lay out our options. Option 1 is to do nothing and just stay the course. This would cause the least disruption to our business, but it doesn't address the fact that we're falling farther and farther behind our numbers. Option 2 is to change our marketing strategy and position ourselves as a good product at a great price. Lowering our prices might help us win additional business in the short term, but it will influence our sales team to sell on price instead of the clear benefits we have versus Gargantuan. Option 3 is to continue with our premium brand marketing strategy and not discount the product. This would enable us to maintain high margins and generate significant profit on each sale, but limit our potential pool of customers who use price as their primary decision-making factor.*

[Resolution] *I believe that this product is our Mona Lisa, our masterpiece. The easy way out would be to do nothing or discount it to grab some low-hanging fruit. Knowing all of you the way I do, I know that you're not that type of team. You're the Special Forces experts of this industry. You're the elite team that's going to stick it to Gargantuan and anyone else who gets in our way as we achieve our goals. Yes, we only have a two-year window to make it happen. But, we're not going to be driven by fear. We're going to be driven by hunger: hunger for success, hunger for the business that we've worked so hard to develop, hunger for the business we deserve. So, we're going to maintain our premium brand marketing strategy. We're not going to discount the product. Initially, we're going to target only benefit-driven decision makers and leave the price-driven customers and their lousy profit margins to Gargantuan.*

[Actions] *In the next two weeks, Marsha and Steve will work together to revise the customer targeting plan, creating a profile of the value-driven customer most likely to pay for the benefits of our high-end product. Steve will then take this profile and sit down with his sales leadership team four weeks from now to identify which customers fit this profile within their respective regions. Steve and his assistant will then develop these revised customer target lists and, six weeks from now, have a meeting with all sales reps to provide guidance on strategically selling value and the policy of no longer discounting. Beginning this quarter, we'll have a functional leadership meeting on the first of each month to ensure that we all are working on strategies that align with each other and help us reach our goals.*

[Theme] We are smaller, so we need to be faster. We have fewer resources, so we need to be more focused. Make no mistake; we are the underdog. Gargantuan is the heavy favorite, but I like our chances, and this launch is crucial to our long-term success. I have here models of a moon rocket—one for each of you. A moon rocket uses about half of its fuel in the first mile of its journey to generate the momentum necessary to break free of the gravity of the earth's atmosphere. We will need to use most of our resources to break Gargantuan's hold on the market and give customers the superior value they deserve. Keep this moon rocket as a reminder of the effort and teamwork we'll need to accomplish this mission.

An effective Strategy Story enables you to combine both acumen and emotion as you convey understanding of the situation and future strategic direction in a memorable way.

1,000-Foot View

Leaders can more effectively use time by:

1. Dedicating chunks of time to a single task
2. Sending fewer e-mails
3. Making time trade-offs using a Time Gauge and Time Trade-Off Matrix

Influence is a person's capacity to be a compelling force on others, and to affect the actions, behaviors, or opinions of others.

One can gain a greater level of commitment to strategy by using social proof. The principle of social proof explains that someone is more likely to behave in a way that is similar to how they see others behave.

A behavior is an observable activity.

Influencing another's behavior comes down to addressing two questions:

1. Is it worth it?
2. Can I do it?

Practice is the systematic repetition of a performance or exercise in order to acquire skill or proficiency. While the applicability of practice is commonly seen in sports, music, and hobbies, the reality is that practice is also integral to success in intellectual pursuits such as strategic thinking.

Three practice principles:

1. Begin with the goal.
2. Break the whole into pieces.
3. Correct with a solution.

A habit is an acquired behavior pattern regularly followed until it has become almost involuntary.

A habit consists of the following three components:

1. Cue (trigger)
2. Routine (behavior)
3. Reward (result)

A strategy conversation is comprised of two types of exchanges: dialogue and discussion.

A dialogue is an exchange of ideas or opinions on a particular issue.

Discussion directs the group toward the actionable strategies, accountability, and implementation that gives the conversation its end result.

The Strategy Story is a format for describing your current situation and the strategic approach you're going to take to lead your team to success. The elements of an effective Strategy Story include the situation, players, challenge, issues, options, resolution, action, and theme.

CONCLUSION

To master a discipline is quite rare,
so too, the ability to rise through the air.

When to Change Strategy

Just as a helicopter pilot monitors his planned course during flight for conditions that would warrant adjustment, we too must monitor our strategic direction to determine when a change in strategy is appropriate. A study of 1,053 companies showed that strategic blunders are at the root of poor performance 81 percent of the time, making them the number-one cause of lost shareholder value.[1] The researchers concluded, "About half the time, the loss of value occurred gradually—over many months or even years if the company took too long to grasp a changed strategic environment or lacked the agility to react."[2] While an action resulting in an error may be highly visible, sometimes it's inaction that is our ultimate undoing. The ability to modify strategy at the right time can literally save or destroy a business. Here is a checklist of five moments when it is critical to evaluate your strategy.

1. **Goals are achieved or changed.** Goals are what you are trying to achieve, and strategy is how you're going to get there. It makes sense then, if the destination changes, so too should the path to get there. As you accomplish goals and establish new ones, changes in resource allocation are often required to keep moving forward. In some cases, goals are modified during the course of the year to reflect changes in the market, competitive landscape,

147

or customer profile. It's important to reflect on the strategy as these changes occur to see if it also needs to be modified.

Ask: Have goals been achieved or changed?

2. **Evolution in customer needs.** The endgame of business strategy is to serve customers' needs in a more profitable way than the competition. But, as the makers of the Polaroid camera, hardcover encyclopedias, and pagers will tell you, customer needs evolve. The leaders skilled in strategic thinking are able to continually generate new insights into the emerging needs of key customers. They can then shape their group's current or future offerings to best meet those evolving needs.

Ask: Have customer needs changed?

3. **Innovation in the market.** Innovation can be described as creating new value for customers. The new value may be technological in nature, but it can also be generated in many other ways including service, experience, marketing, process, etc. It may be earth shattering, or it may be minor in nature. The key is to keep a tight pulse on your market, customers, and competitors to understand when innovation, or new value, is being delivered and by whom. Once that's confirmed, assess your goals and strategies to determine if they need to be adjusted based on this new level of value in the market.

Ask: Is there new value in the market?

4. **Competitors change the perception of value.** For many years, fast food was fast food. Burgers, tacos, chicken, pizza, and hot dogs were the standard fare. Within each category, there was greater similarity between competing offerings than distinction. As Subway entered a period of rapid expansion through franchising, it began to promote a healthier fast food. Eventually, they used a spokesman who lost weight on the "Subway diet" to lead the campaign, and the fast food arena slowly started to change. People who never really considered the nutritional aspect of their fast-food meals were now faced with healthier choices. Subway

crafted a new perception of value in the market. While we'd like to believe that people choose products and services based on the actual merits of the offerings, we know that this isn't always the case. Shaping the perceived value of an offering through marketing campaigns, social media, celebrity endorsements, and so on is a powerful weapon or threat, depending on your position.

Ask: Have competitors changed the perception of value in the market?

5. **Capabilities grow or decline.** A final consideration when determining whether or not to change strategies deals with what's under your own roof. Having led strategic planning sessions for the past 15 years, I've observed how challenging it can be for organizations to honestly evaluate their own capabilities relative to competitors. One indication is compiling a meandering laundry list of 15 strengths during the SWOT Analysis exercise (which lists an organization's strengths, weaknesses, opportunities, and threats). However, objective assessment of the group's capabilities relative to the competition is a starting point. If your capabilities have significantly grown, it may open up new strategies for capitalizing on opportunities to increase profits. If your capabilities have declined, it may call for new strategies to neutralize competitor initiatives or to exit the market.

Ask: What is the state of your capabilities?

Fire Prevention

As you consider the five key factors necessary when reviewing strategy to determine any changes in course, keep in mind that fires are generally not a reason to change strategy. However, you may have some managers who are all too eager to don the helmet and hose and swoop in to save the day through urgent but unimportant tasks. The problem with this firefighting mentality is the opportunity costs it bleeds from your business. Time, talent, and budget spent on fighting urgent but unimportant fires are resources that can't be properly invested elsewhere to support the successful execution of your strategy. Research with 197 global companies on the reasons for the underperformance of strategy found that the biggest contributing factor is, "the failure to have the right resources in the right place at the right time."[3] Taking a few hours here and there each week to attend to fires might not seem like a big deal, but it is. Take those few hours a week and multiply that by the number of managers in the organization. It's quickly evident how thousands of hours a year can be wasted with no way to regain those precious resources.

It's recommended that at least twice a year you conduct a Fire Prevention exercise with your management team. The Fire Prevention exercise is designed to help you put out some of the recurring fires by taking action on the things that ignite them. The first step in the exercise is to identify the fires: urgent but unimportant activities that are not a part of your plan, but require a resource investment. The second step is to have a strategy conversation with all of the people involved in that fire to shed light on its cause. The third and final step is to create an approach to stop the fire from consuming your resources. There are three potential actions when dealing with a fire:

1. **Control:** Invest resources the first time (and only the first time) a fire appears in order to control it, prior to further analysis.
2. **Delegate:** Pass the resource investment requirement to a group or person with the appropriate accountability for such an event.
3. **Prevent:** Determine and eliminate the root cause.

Examples of internal fires include:

- Senior leaders demanding lists or reports that require time, labor, and energy to put together, versus those that can be automatically generated
- Flavor-of-the-month initiatives that aren't directly related to people's strategic plans
- Attendance on conference calls that have no direct business value for the participant

Table 4.1   Fire Prevention

Fire	Cause	Action (Control, Delegate, Prevent)

Examples of external fires include:

- The same customer continually asking for activities to be performed in a much shorter time frame than normal
- Requests for proposal (RFP) that don't match up with your business acquisition criteria
- People outside the organization seeking teleconferences or meetings to discuss partnerships or alliances without first providing sufficient business rationale

The template in Table 4.1 will enable you to track your Fire Prevention efforts over the course of time, and decipher patterns of activity.

Tactical Evaluation Matrix

Tactics are another factor that can potentially consume huge sums of resources without yielding much in the way of results. Tactics are the tangible actions behind how we accomplish goals and objectives. They represent the specific items you put time and money into in order to carry out the general strategic approach to achieving the goals. Sales brochures, training binders, iPads, apps, and educational programs are examples of tactics. Some managers take the more-is-more approach to tactics, filling their plans with all available tactics so they can't be faulted for not including a tactic if they didn't meet their goals. While it may provide political protection internally, the laundry list approach to tactics does little to advance the effective and efficient use of one's resources. Apple CEO Tim Cook says, "And we argue and debate like crazy about what we're not going to do, because we know that we can only do a few things great. That means not doing a bunch of things that would be really good and really fun. That's a part of our base principle, that we will only do a few things."[4]

Even the soundest of strategies can be rendered powerless if the tactics employed to realize them are ineffective, undifferentiated, or overwhelming in number. As a senior leader, it's important to convey to your managers that all tactics are not created equal. Just as managers must be discerning in how to articulate strategy for a product or service, they must also realize that each expenditure of resources on a tactic either brings value to customers or wastes the organization's resources. While the day-to-day implementation of tactics may not be your job, it's critical to educate the people whose job it is to ensure they're using resources effectively to create only value-generating tactics—even if it means eliminating something.

The Tactical Evaluation Matrix is a tool used to assess the tactics of the business on two parameters: efficacy with customers, and differentiation from competitors. Efficacy with customers is determined by two factors:

1. The extent to which the tactic is embraced and utilized by internal customers (company personnel) to influence external customers in the selection and use of your offerings
2. The importance external customers place on the tactic when it's received

The second criterion of the Tactical Evaluation Matrix is differentiation from the competition. In other words, do external customers

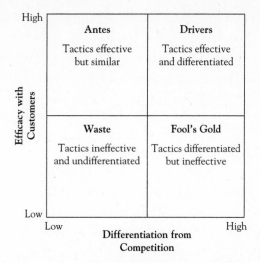

Figure 4.1 Tactical Evaluation Matrix

perceive a positive difference in value from this tactic relative to tactics the competition provide to them?

Figure 4.1 provides an example of the Tactical Evaluation Matrix. To use this tool, first create a list of all of the tactics that you are currently investing in. Then plot those tactics within the matrix based on their level of efficacy with customers (low to high) and differentiation from the competition (low to high). Each tactic will fall into one of the following quadrants:

Waste: Tactics ineffective and undifferentiated

Antes: Tactics effective but similar

Fool's Gold: Tactics differentiated but ineffective

Drivers: Tactics effective and differentiated

Strategy Launch Review

The U.S. Army introduced the After-Action Review (AAR) to create a process for continuous learning from initiatives. Developed by the National Training Center in 1981, the AAR's original use in the army's Opposing Force (OPFOR) has expanded to most military services in one form or another.[5] The AAR provides a checkpoint for cultivating the knowledge and insights gained from initiatives by addressing four points:[6]

1. What were our intended results?
2. What were our actual results?
3. What caused our results?
4. What will we sustain or improve?

We can modify this concept to improve our strategy efforts in non-military organizations as well. Prior to launching a new strategic initiative, have the team leader conduct a Before Strategy Launch Review (BSLR). The BSLR should be a facilitated strategy conversation around the following three questions:

1. What is the goal of the initiative?
2. What is the strategic approach being used to achieve this goal?
3. What are the key challenges to successful implementation of the initiative and how will we address them?

Once the strategy initiative has been completed, modified, or discontinued, the After Strategy Launch Review (ASLR) should take place. The ASLR answers three questions:

1. What happened?
2. How or why did it happen?
3. What did we learn from it?

The leader should then take the group's input on these questions and summarize the results of the Strategy Launch Initiative. These summaries should include both the positive—what went right and what we did well—and the negative—what areas need improvement. The results of each ASLR should be kept together and reviewed quarterly to generate recommendations on how to improve the overall strategy initiative process. What's working? What's not working? Are there any trends or patterns? Are people educated on and engaged in the process? The ASLR not only provides an opportunity to improve the activities that drive the implementation of strategic initiatives, but it also enables managers to continually improve the thinking that goes into the development of their strategic initiatives in the first place.

Strategy Scaffold

A number of man-made masterpieces, including the Egyptian pyramids and Michelangelo's painting of the ceiling of the Sistine Chapel, were made possible by the use of scaffolds. A scaffold is a temporary structure used to elevate people to a higher place in order to work. Drive by any number of structures being built or refurbished, and there's a good chance you'll see scaffolding supporting people to work at greater heights. Scaffolds range from the relatively simple ones used to work on a home project to the grander versions for assisting projects as important as enhancements to the Statue of Liberty.

Mastering the three disciplines of advanced strategic thinking—coalesce, compete, and champion—requires the ability to work at a higher level. The Strategy Scaffold provides leaders with a one-page tool to build, adjust, and communicate the foundational elements of the business. A crucial part of the leader's strategic skill set is to be able to clearly and concisely convey the essence of the business. A study of 1,000 global companies confirmed this importance as the researchers concluded: "The only competency viewed as essential for CEOs, COOs, and CFOs alike was developing an accurate and comprehensive overview of the business."[7] The Strategy Scaffold provides leaders with the framework to see how the foundational elements of their business connect and support one another. It also can illuminate cracks in the foundation of the business, which if left unnoticed, could lead to its eventual collapse. The Strategy Scaffold consists of the following three planks:

1. **Purpose:** The intent of the business represented by the following elements:
   o Mission: Current purpose; clear, concise, and enduring statement of the reasons for an organization's existence today

o Vision: Future purpose; provides a mental picture of the aspirations an organization is working toward

o Values: Guide purpose; ideals and principles that influence the thoughts and actions of an organization, and define its character

2. **Business Model:** A structural description of how the organization creates, delivers, and captures value.

Create:

o Core Competency: Primary area of expertise (what you know)

o Capabilities: Activities performed with key resources (what you do)

o Value Proposition: Rationale for the offering (customer, need/job, approach, benefit)

Deliver:

o Value Chain: Configuration of capabilities to provide value (how you do it)

o Channels: Customer access points for offerings (where you offer it)

Capture:

o Price Position: Amount customers pay for the offering relative to alternative options (low, moderate, premium)

3. **Plan:** The strategic direction of the business.

o Goals: What you are trying to achieve (general)

o Objectives: What you are trying achieve (specific)

o Strategy: How you will achieve the goals/objectives (general)

o Tactics: How you will achieve the goals/objectives (specific)

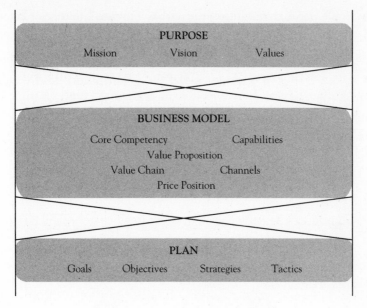

Figure 4.2   Strategy Scaffold

Figure 4.2 represents the Strategy Scaffold framework.

Strategic I Am

Pick-up sticks is a game many played as children. A bundle of sticks roughly six inches long are held in a loose bunch and released on a table top, falling in random disarray. Each player then takes a turn removing a stick from the pile, with the goal of not moving or disturbing the remaining ones. Unfortunately, in many organizations, strategy development resembles a game of pick-up sticks. Unable to escape the whirlwind of daily activities, managers annually throw together a strategic planning session comprised of a series of random questions and a SWOT analysis, for good measure. With no rationale as to their sequencing or practical application, this jumble of jargon and templates can best be described as a Pick-up strategy session. People leave these sessions with a frustrated, unfulfilled sense of having done little thinking in an unproductive way that generated no real changes in the business.

As we've seen throughout the book, elevated levels of strategic thinking can be guided by a coherent and methodical framework consisting of concepts and tools to help you achieve your business goals. The Three Disciplines of *Advanced* Strategic Thinking provide a concise, yet comprehensive way for leaders to raise their level of thought in setting strong strategic direction for the business. They are as follows:

1. **Coalesce:** Fusing together insights to create an innovative business model
2. **Compete:** Creating a system of strategy to achieve competitive advantage
3. **Champion:** Leading others to think and act strategically to execute strategy

Mastering these disciplines will take time. Revamping business models, revisiting value propositions, enhancing value chains, mining the market for innovation, assessing competitive advantage, influencing others to buy in, building new habits, facilitating strategy conversations, and designing a Strategy Scaffold all require a significant investment of time, energy, and commitment. It won't be easy and it certainly won't come without risks. Saying no to some potential customers, not saying yes to every internal request that comes across your desk, and forgoing promising opportunities because they don't fit with your strategy will open you up to risk. Having the intellectual prowess and the sheer guts to make these trade-offs defines the truly strategic leader.

What's your end game? When your career comes to a close, where will you be? What shape will your business be in? How will your colleagues, employees, and customers describe you? Most important, how will you assess your run? Contrary to popular belief, it's not about the little things. It's about how you create the defining moments that shape the trajectory of a team, a business, a life. It's about coalescing insights into competitive advantages that you champion. It's about rising above the fray and seeing things others don't. And you can make that happen, if you're willing to elevate.

A common maple seed, like those you tossed up into the air as a kid and then watched as they spun to the ground, uses the same principle of autorotation as a helicopter does when it descends. In fact, single-engine helicopters are designed with this autorotation principle in mind so they can flutter to the ground safely in the event of engine failure. The maple seed's illustration of the principle behind helicopter flight is just one example of how something complex can be made simple. Leonardo da Vinci, whose design of the aerial screw inspired the future development of the helicopter said, "Simplicity is the ultimate sophistication." Great strategy should be simple, maybe even as simple as a Dr. Seuss book. And if Dr. Seuss had been a strategist, I think he may have written something like this:

Strategic I Am

I am strategic. Strategic I am.

Do you like to think strategically?

I do not like to think strategically,

not in an office, not in a tree.

It's more fun to think tactically,

stuff I can touch, stuff I can see.

I do not like to think strategically,

I haven't the time to be so leisurely.

Setting good plans, I'll leave to others.

Gotta check my e-mail. Even in bed, under the covers.

No, I do not like to think strategically,

I prefer the adrenaline rush of mindless reactivity.

You do not like to think strategically,

so you say. Try it, try it, and you may.

Say! I do like to think strategically.

While others around me only fight fires,

I focus my resources, taking my business higher.

I schedule time, just to think.

Now my goals and strategies are in perfect sync.

Thank you, thank you!

Strategic I am.

1,000-Foot View

Five moments signaling the need for a strategy review:

1. Goals are achieved or changed
2. Evolution in customer needs
3. Innovation in the market
4. Competitors change the perception of value
5. Capabilities grow or decline

Three potential ways to deal with recurring fires:

1. Control
2. Delegate
3. Prevent

The Tactical Evaluation Matrix is a tool used to assess the tactics of the business on two parameters: efficacy with customers, and differentiation from competitors.

The Before Strategy Launch Review (BSLR) asks three questions:

1. What is the goal of the initiative?
2. What is the strategic approach being used to achieve this goal?
3. What are the key challenges to successful implementation of the initiative and how will we address them?

The After Strategy Launch Review (ASLR) should take place when a strategy initiative has been completed, modified, or discontinued. The ASLR answers three questions:

1. What happened?
2. How or why did it happen?
3. What did we learn from it?

The Strategy Scaffold provides leaders with a one-page tool to build, adjust, and communicate the foundational elements of the business including purpose, business model, and plan.

NOTES

Introduction

1. *Merriam-Webster's Dictionary,* "elevate," Merriam-Webster Online, accessed November 23, 2013.
2. Chris Zook and James Allen, *Repeatability* (Boston: Harvard Business Review Press, 2012).
3. James Chiles, *The God Machine* (New York: Bantam Books, 2007).
4. Adam Hartung, *Create Marketplace Disruption* (Upper Saddle River, NJ: FT Press, 2009).
5. Matthew Olson, Derek van Bever, and Seth Verry, "When Growth Stalls," *Harvard Business Review,* March 2008.
6. Ibid.
7. Shara Tibken, "Sprint Loses More Customers," *Wall Street Journal,* July 29, 2011.
8. MSNBC.com Staff, "Final Chapter, Borders to Close Remaining Stores," *NBCnews.com,* July 18, 2011.
9. Ram Charan, "Why Companies Fail," *Fortune,* May 27, 2002.
10. Anita McGahan and Michael Porter, "The Emergence and Sustainability of Abnormal Profits," *Strategic Organization* 1, 2003.
11. Paul Carroll and Chunka Mui, "7 Ways to Fail Big," *Harvard Business Review,* September 2008.
12. Michael Totty, "The View from the CIO's Office," *Wall Street Journal,* April 25, 2011.
13. Bernard Wirtz, "Strategy in High-Velocity Environments," *Long Range Planning* 40, 2007.
14. Edward Bowman, "Does Corporate Strategy Matter?" *Strategic Management Journal* 22, 2001.
15. Michael Birshan, "Creating More Value with Corporate Strategy," *McKinsey Global Survey Results,* December 2010.

16. Roger Martin, "The Execution Trap," *Harvard Business Review*, July-August 2010.
17. Robert Kaplan and David Norton, "The Office of Strategy Management," *Harvard Business Review*, October 2005.
18. Stephen Covey, *The 8th Habit* (New York: Free Press, 2004).
19. Alan Deutschman, *Change or Die* (New York: Regan, 2007).
20. Alexandra Wolfe, "Weekend Confidential: Howard Schultz," *Wall Street Journal*, September 28–29, 2013.
21. Richard Rumelt, "The Perils of Bad Strategy," *McKinsey Quarterly* 1, 2011.
22. Bob Garratt, *Developing Strategic Thought: Rediscovering the Art of Direction-Giving* (London: McGraw-Hill, 1995).
23. Rich Horwath, *Deep Dive: The Proven Method for Building Strategy, Focusing Your Resources and Taking Smart Action* (Austin: Greenleaf Book Group Press, 2009).
24. Richard Rosen, "CEOs Misperceive Top Team's Performance," *Harvard Business Review*, September 2007.
25. A. G. Lafley and Roger Martin, *Playing to Win* (Boston: Harvard Business Review Press, 2013).
26. Donley Townsend, "Engaging the Board of Directors on Strategy," *Strategy & Leadership* 35, no. 5, 2007.
27. Schumpeter, "Too Much Buzz," *The Economist*, December 31, 2011.
28. Chris Bradley, "Have You Tested Your Strategy Lately?" *McKinsey Quarterly*, January 2011.
29. Sun Tzu, James Clavell, ed., *The Art of War* (New York: Delacorte Press, 1983).
30. Scott Martin, "LinkedIn goes wide with media content," *USA Today*, September 26, 2013.
31. Nina Kruschwitz and Knut Haanaes, "First Look: Highlights from the Third Annual Sustainability Global Executive Survey," *MIT Sloan Management Review*, Fall 2011.
32. Michael Raynor and Mumtaz Ahmed, "Three Rules for Making a Company Truly Great," *Harvard Business Review*, April 2013.
33. Adi Ignatius, "We Had to Own the Mistakes," *Harvard Business Review*, July-August 2010.
34. Barry Jaruzelski, "The Global Innovation 1000: Making Ideas Work," *strategy + business*, 69, Winter 2012.
35. Ingrid Bonn, "Developing Strategic Thinking as a Core Competency," *Management Decision* 39, 2001.
36. J. P. Donlon, "Best Companies for Leaders," *Chief Executive Magazine*, January/February 2009.
37. Alina Dizik, "Are They Worth It?" *Wall Street Journal*, September 30, 2008.

38. Michael Birshan and Jayanti Kar, "Becoming More Strategic: Three Tips for Any Executive," *McKinsey Quarterly*, July 2012.
39. Patricia Sellers, "The Queen of Pop," *Fortune*, September 28, 2009.
40. Kathy Chu, "Yum Brands CEO takes global view on fast food," *USA Today*, February 27, 2012.
41. Jennifer Pellet, "Study Says CEOs Disappoint as Board Members, But Numbers Tell a Different Story," *Chief Executive Magazine*, November/December 2011.
42. Boris Groysberg, "The New Path to the C-Suite," *Harvard Business Review*, March 2011.

Discipline #1: Coalesce

1. James Chiles, *The God Machine* (New York: Bantam Books, 2007).
2. *Merriam-Webster's Dictionary*, "pattern," Merriam-Webster Online, accessed November 23, 2013.
3. Kenneth Andrews, *The Concept of Corporate Strategy* (Homewood, IL: Irwin, 1971).
4. Ibid.
5. Donald Sull, "How to Thrive in Turbulent Markets," *Harvard Business Review*, February 2009.
6. Stephen Hall, "How to Put Your Money Where Your Strategy Is," *McKinsey Quarterly*, March 2012.
7. Ibid.
8. Rita McGrath, "Transient Advantage," *Harvard Business Review*, June 2013.
9. Andreas Kramvis, "Breaking Strategic Inertia," *McKinsey Quarterly*, April 2012.
10. Fritjof Capra, *The Web of Life: A New Scientific Understanding of Living Systems* (New York: Anchor Books, 1997).
11. Donella Meadows, *Thinking in Systems* (White River Junction, VT: Chelsea Green Publishing, 2008).
12. David Kaplan, "Chipotle's Growth Machine," *Fortune*, September 26, 2011.
13. Martin Reeves and Mike Deimler, "Adaptability: The New Competitive Advantage," *Harvard Business Review*, July-August 2011.
14. Michael Porter, "What is Strategy?" *Harvard Business Review*, November-December 1996.
15. Peter Newcomb, "Reid Hoffman," *Wall Street Journal Magazine*, July/August 2011.
16. W. Chan Kim and Renee Mauborgne, *Blue Ocean Strategy* (Boston: Harvard Business School Press, 2005).

17. Eddie Yoon and Linda Deeken, "Why It Pays to Be a Category Creator," *Harvard Business Review*, March 2013.

18. Rob Norton, "The Thought Leader Interview: Henry Chesbrough," *strategy + business*, 63, Summer 2011.

19. Michael Cusumano, *Staying Power* (New York: Oxford University Press, 2010).

20. Alexander Osterwalder and Yves Pigneur, *Business Model Generation* (Hoboken, NJ: John Wiley & Sons, 2010).

21. Zhenya Lindgart, "Business Model Innovation," *Boston Consulting Group*, December 2009.

22. Geoff Colvin, "Your Business Model Doesn't Work Anymore," *Fortune*, February 25, 2013.

23. C. K. Prahalad and Gary Hamel, "The Core Competence of the Corporation," *Harvard Business Review*, May-June 1990.

24. Robert Kaplan and David Norton, "Having Trouble with Your Strategy? Then Map It," *Harvard Business Review*, September-October 2000.

25. Mark Johnson, Clayton Christensen, and Henning Kagermann, "Reinventing Your Business Model," *Harvard Business Review*, December 2008.

26. Adam Lashinsky, "Jeff Bezos: The Ultimate Disrupter," *Fortune*, December 3, 2012.

27. Keniche Ohmae, "Getting Back to Strategy," *Harvard Business Review*, November-December 1988.

28. Theodore Levitt, "Marketing Success Through Differentiation," *Harvard Business Review*, January-Februrary, 1980.

29. James Dyson, *Against the Odds* (New York: Texere, New York, 2003).

30. Todd Zenger, "What is the Theory of Your Firm?" *Harvard Business Review*, June 2013.

31. Michael Porter, *Competitive Advantage* (New York: The Free Press,, 1985).

32. Alexander Osterwalder and & Yves Pigneur, *Business Model Generation* (Hoboken, NJ: John Wiley & Sons, 2010).

33. Richard Rumelt, "How Much Does Industry Matter?" *Strategic Management Journal* 12, March 1991.

34. Paul Rubin, "A Tutorial for the President on 'Profit Maximization'," *Wall Street Journal*, May 24, 2012.

35. Jamie Bonomo and Andy Pasternak, "Unlocking Profitability in the Complex Company," *Mercer Management Journal* 18, 2004.

36. Michael Raynor and Mumtaz Ahmed, "Up in the Air," *The Conference Board Review*, Spring 2013.

37. Jeffrey McCracken, "At Ford, the 'Outsider' is Optimistic," *Wall Street Journal*, July 23, 2007.

38. Allen Webb, "Starbuck's Quest for Healthy Growth: An Interview with Howard Schulz," *McKinsey Quarterly* 2011.
39. Matthew Olson, Derek van Bever, and Seth Verry, "When Growth Stalls," *Harvard Business Review*, March 2008.
40. David Henry, "Mergers: Why Most Big Deals Don't Pay Off," *BusinessWeek*, October 14, 2002.
41. Mehrdad Baghai, Stephen Coley, and David White, *The Alchemy of Growth* (London: Basic Books, 1999).
42. Jonah Lehrer, "How to Be Creative," *Wall Street Journal*, March 10–11, 2012.
43. Michael Hsu, "James Dyson," *Wall Street Journal*, February 9–10, 2013.
44. James Dyson, *Against the Odds* (New York: Texere, 2003).
45. Geoffrey Moore, *Dealing with Darwin* (New York: Portfolio, 2005).
46. Nitin Nohria and Anthony Mayo, "Zeitgeist Leadership," *Harvard Business Review*, October 2005.
47. Moore, *Dealing with Darwin*.
48. Michael Treacy and Fred Wiersema, *The Discipline of Market Leaders* (New York: Perseus, 1995).
49. Clayton Christensen, *The Innovator's Dilemma* (Boston: Harvard Business School Press, 1997).

Discipline #2: Compete

1. Rona Goffen, *Renaissance Rivals: Michelangelo, Leonardo, Raphael, Titian* (New Haven, CT: Yale University Press, 2004).
2. *Merriam-Webster's Dictionary*, "compete," Merriam-Webster Online, accessed November 23, 2013.
3. Po Bronson and Ashley Merryman, *Top Dog: The Science of Winning and Losing* (New York: Twelve, 2013).
4. Ibid.
5. Jonah Berger, "If You Want to Win, Tell Your Team It's Losing (a Little)," *Harvard Business Review*, October 2011.
6. Ibid.
7. Jill Rosenfeld, "The Art of Business," *Fast Company*, August 2001.
8. Daniel Kahneman and Amos Tversky, "The Psychology of Preferences," *Scientific American*, 160, 1982.
9. Stephen Hall, "How to Put Your Money Where Your Strategy Is," *McKinsey Quarterly*, March 2012.
10. Donald Sull, "How to Thrive in Turbulent Markets," *Harvard Business Review*, February 2009.

11. Stephen Hall, "How to Put Your Money Where Your Strategy Is."
12. Adam Bluestein, "The Rules: Do Less," *Inc.*, February 2013.
13. Michael Raynor and Mumtaz Ahmed, "Three Rules for Making a Company Truly Great," *Harvard Business Review*, April 2013.
14. Chris Zook and James Allen, *Repeatability* (Boston: Harvard Business Review Press, 2012).
15. Karl Greenfeld, "Let the Games Begin," *Businessweek*, July 18, 2013.
16. "2013 State of the Industry: Bottled water," *Beverage Industry*, July 10, 2013.
17. Theodore Levitt, "Marketing Success through Differentiation—Of Anything," *Harvard Business Review*, January-February 1980.
18. Zook and Allen, *Repeatability*.
19. Robert Hof, "How to Hit a Moving Target," *Businessweek*, August 20, 2006.
20. Chris Bradley and Eric Matson, "Putting Strategies to the Test," *McKinsey Quarterly*, January 2011.
21. Kevin Coyne, "Predicting Your Competitor's Reaction," *Harvard Business Review*, April 2009.
22. "Thoughts on Chess," *Forbes*, February 22, 2012.
23. Michael Porter, *Competitive Strategy* (New York: The Free Press, 1980).
24. Michael Porter, "The Five Competitive Forces that Shape Strategy," *Harvard Business Review*, January 2008.
25. Mark Bergen and Margaret Peteraf, "Competitor Identification and Competitor Analysis," *Managerial and Decision Economics* 23, June-August 2002.
26. Alan Deutschman, *Change or Die* (New York: Regan, 2007).
27. Steve Lavalle, "Analytics and the New Path to Value," *MIT Sloan Management Review*, Winter 2011.

Discipline #3: Champion

1. Frankki Bevins and Aaron De Smet, "Making Time Management the Organization's Priority," *McKinsey Quarterly* 1, 2013.
2. Julian Birkinshaw and Jordan Cohen, "Make Time for the Work That Matters," *Harvard Business Review*, September 2013.
3. Issie Lapowsky, "Get More Done," *Inc.*, April 2013.
4. Henry Mintzberg and Peter Todd, "The Offline Executive," *strategy + business*, 69, Winter 2012.
5. Heike Bruch and Sumantra Ghoshal, "Beware the Busy Manager," *Harvard Business Review*, February 2002.
6. "The Multitasking Paradox," *Harvard Business Review*, March 2013.
7. Derek Dean and Caroline Webb, "Recovering from Information Overload," *McKinsey Quarterly* 1, 2011.

8. Stuart Crainer, "Clocking In," *Business Strategy Review* 4, 2011.

9. Bevins and De Smet, "Making Time Management the Organization's Priority."

10. Peter Bregman, "A Personal Approach to Organizational Time Management," *McKinsey Quarterly* 1, 2013.

11. Jeff Weiner, "The Importance of Scheduling Nothing," *LinkedIn*, April 10, 2013.

12. Bevins and De Smet, "Making Time Management the Organization's Priority."

13. Stuart Crainer, "Clocking In."

14. Jeff Weiner, "The Importance of Scheduling Nothing."

15. John Byrne, "The 12 Greatest Entrepreneurs of Our Time," *Fortune*, April 9, 2012.

16. Chris Zook and James Allen, *Repeatability* (Boston: Harvard Business Review Press, 2012).

17. Chris Anderson, "EM," *Wired*, November 2012.

18. Alison Wellner, "The Time Trap," *Inc.*, June 2004.

19. Paul Hemp, "Death by Information Overload," *Harvard Business Review*, September 2009.

20. Chris Brown, Andrew Killick, and Karen Renaud, "To Reduce E-mail, Start at the Top," *Harvard Business Review*, September 2013.

21. *Merriam-Webster's Dictionary*, "influence," Merriam-Webster Online, accessed November 23, 2013.

22. Dan Pink, *To Sell Is Human* (New York: Riverhead Books, 2012).

23. Charles Galunic, "How to Help Employees 'Get' Strategy," *Harvard Business Review*, December 2012.

24. R. Timothy Breene, Paul Nunes, and Walter Shill, "The Chief Strategy Officer," *Harvard Business Review*, October 2007.

25. Fiona Czerniawska, "Executing Strategy: Lessons from Private Equity," *Strategy Magazine*, September 2007.

26. Ellen Langer, A. Blank, and B. Chanowitz, "The Mindlessness of Ostensibly Thoughtful Action: The Role of 'Placebic' Information in Interpersonal Interaction," *Journal of Personality and Social Psychology* 36, 1978.

27. Robert Cialdini, *Influence: Science and Practice* (Boston: Allyn and Bacon, 2001).

28. Jennifer Mueller, Shimul Melwani, and Jack Goncalo, "The Bias Against Creativity: Why People Desire but Reject Creative Ideas," *Psychological Science* 23, 2012.

29. Dan Pink, *To Sell Is Human*.

30. Brian Wansink, *Mindless Eating: Why We Eat More than We Think* (New York: Bantam Books, 2006).

31. George Anders, "Jeff Bezos Gets It," *Forbes*, April 23, 2012.
32. Adam Lashinsky, "Jeff Bezos: The Ultimate Disrupter," *Fortune*, December 3, 2012.
33. David Myers, "The Power and Perils of Intuition," *Scientific American Mind*, June/July 2007.
34. David Dusenbery, *Living at Micro Scale: The Unexpected Physics of Being Small* (Cambridge, MA: Harvard University Press, 2009).
35. Kerry Patterson, Joseph Grenny, David Maxfield, Ron McMillan, and Al Switzler, *Influencer: The Power to Change Anything* (New York: McGraw-Hill, 2008).
36. Doug Lemov, *Teach Like a Champion* (San Francisco: Jossey-Bass, 2010).
37. Mihaly Csikszentmihalyi, *Flow: The Psychology of Optimal Experience* (New York: Harper and Row, 1990).
38. Rich Horwath, *Deep Dive: The Proven Method for Building Strategy, Focusing Your Resources and Taking Smart Action* (Austin: Greenleaf Book Group Press, 2009).
39. *Merriam-Webster's Dictionary*, "inspire."
40. Jim Loehr and Tony Schwartz, *The Power of Full Engagement* (New York: Free Press, 2003).
41. Michael Laff, "Senior Managers Absent from the Training Table," *T + D*, July 2007.
42. *Merriam-Webster's Dictionary*, "practice."
43. Roger Parloff, "On History's Stage: Chief Justice John Roberts Jr.," *Fortune*, January 17, 2011.
44. Ibid.
45. Doug Lemov, Erica Woolway, and Katie Yezzi, *Practice Perfect: 42 Rules for Getting Better at Getting Better* (San Francisco: Jossey-Bass, 2012).
46. Ibid.
47. Patterson, et. al. *Influencer: The Power to Change Anything.*
48. Daniel Coyle, *The Talent Code* (New York: Bantam Books, 2009).
49. Ibid.
50. Ibid.
51. Roland Tharp and Ron Gallimore, "Basketball's John Wooden: What a Coach Can Teach a Teacher," *Psychology Today* 9, 1976.
52. Roland Tharp and Ron Gallimore, "What a Coach Can Teach a Teacher, 1975–2004: Reflections and Reanalysis of John Wooden's Teaching Practices," *The Sport Psychologist* 18, 2004.
53. *Merriam-Webster's Dictionary*, "habit."
54. Ann Graybiel, "The Basal Ganglia and Chunking of Action Repertoires," *Neurobiology of Learning and Memory* 70, 1998.
55. Charles Duhigg, *The Power of Habit* (New York: Random House, 2012).

56. William Isaacs, "Dialogic Leadership," *The Systems Thinker*, February 1999.

57. Ram Charan, "Conquering a Culture of Indecision," *Harvard Business Review*, April 2001.

58. Donald Sull, "Closing the Gap Between Strategy and Execution," *MIT Sloan Management Review*, Summer 2007.

59. Bruce Harreld, "Dynamic Capabilities at IBM," *California Management Review*, 49, no. 4, Summer 2007.

60. Gordon Shaw, Robert Brown, and Philip Bromiley, "Strategic Stories: How 3M is Rewriting Business Planning," *Harvard Business Review*, May-June 1998.

61. Michael Carriger, "Narrative vs. PowerPoint: For Leaders, It May Not be a Matter of Fact," *Strategy & Leadership* 38, no. 2, 2010.

62. Ibid.

63. Adam Lashinsky, "Jeff Bezos: The Ultimate Disrupter," *Fortune*, December 3, 2012.

64. Eileen Roche, "Words for the Wise," *Harvard Business Review*, January 2001.

Conclusion

1. Christopher Dann, Matthew Le Merle, and Christopher Pencavel, "The Lesson of Lost Value," *strategy + business*, 69, Winter 2012.

2. Ibid.

3. Michael Mankins and Richard Steele, "Turning Great Strategy into Great Performance," *Harvard Business Review*, July-August 2005.

4. Josh Tyrangiel, "Tim Cook's Freshman Year," *Businessweek*, December 6, 2012.

5. Marilyn Darling, Charles Parry, and Joseph Moore, "Learning in the Thick of It," *Harvard Business Review*, July-August 2005.

6. Ibid.

7. Howard Stevens, "The Leadership Paradox," *Chief Learning Officer*, April 2012.

INDEX

ACKNOWLEDGMENTS

Thanks to my wife Anne for her spirit and support, and to our children Luke and Jessica, for filling our home with love and laughter. I am eternally grateful to my parents, Jan and Rich, and sister Sharon for the blessings that come from growing up in a healthy, happy family.

I'd like to thank the following business leaders for sharing their wisdom and insights with me during our work together:

Chris Anderson, Chris Bevel, Craig Besler, Elaine Bittner, Jim Blount, Sam Brandes, Frank Brletich, Kevin Buckle, Vince Caldwell, Tony Casciano, Jerry Casey, Dawn Ciambriello, Kevin Combs, Peter Cooke, Cyndi Davis, Andrew de Guttadauro, Heather DeMyers, Steve Denault, Heidi Devine, Brenda Devlin, Domenick DiCindio, Bryan Distefano, Don Doddridge, Michelle Dolieslager, Bryan Downey, Lisa Dreher, Darrell Fick, Jim Floyd, Tom Fordonski, Valerie Gerbino, Kevin Goodwin, Dean Gregory, Jeff Haas, David Hammond, Robert Hanf, Paul Hardy, Melissa Hauser, LynAnn Henderson, Dale Hicks, Matt Hodson, Todd Hunt, Troy Iaconis, Jim Immormino, Jim Johnson, Dana Jones, Mary Jones, Ranndy Kellogg, Carolyn Kircher, Letty Klutz, Oliver Konarkowski, Rick Kosturko, Kevin Kutler, Steve Lamb, Kirk Leeds, Cathy Leggette, Dan Linden, Richard Locke, Cheryl Lubbert, Rick Marcotte, Keith Martino, Bill McDonough, Mike McMasters, Michael Mehler, Brian Meinken, Pete Menary, Greg Moisan, Bill Mosteller, Kevin Mullins, Taylor Neely, Tim O'Connor, Cinda Orr, Greg Palko, Bob Palumbo, Joe Palumbo, Karen Parkyn-Michael, Laura Perkins, Mike Pietsch, Don Pogorzelski, Kris Porter, Jeff Potts, Pallav Raval, Rick Rice, Perry Robinson, Cheryl Ronk, Chris Rottenberk,

Sharon Ryan, Jeffrey Sanfilippo, Jasper Sanfilippo Jr., Sid Sawhney, Janet Schijns, Rob Schneider, Bud Scholl, Bob Schruender, Steve Sesterhenn, Regina Shanklin, Patrick Silvey, Dale Snyder, Scott Shuster, Julie Slingerman, Dario Solano, Rich Stewart, Jackie Sturm, Andy Surtz, Mark Sutter, Joe Talanges, Christie Tarantino, Norman Tashash, Dave Taylor, Jeff Taylor, Phil Tegeler, Jay Tibbets, Al Topin, Kyle Valby, Mike Valentine, Chris Varcoe, Rich Verde, Christine Waite, Terry Walsh, John Wandishin, Michael Williams, Carl Willis, and John Zgombic.

Finally, a special thanks to the amazing group at Wiley for their commitment to excellence throughout the publishing process: Brian Neill, Charlotte Maiorana, Deborah Schindlar, Peter Knox, Amy Packard, and the entire team.

ABOUT THE AUTHOR

Rich Horwath is a *New York Times*, *Wall Street Journal*, and *USA Today* bestselling author on strategy. As the CEO of the Strategic Thinking Institute, Rich leads executive teams through the strategy process and has helped more than 50,000 managers around the world develop their strategic thinking skills. A former chief strategy officer and professor of strategy, he brings both real-world experience and practical expertise to help both companies and leaders build their strategic capabilities. Rich and his work have appeared on ABC, CBS, CNBC, CNN, NBC, and FOX. He is recognized in the textbook *Strategy in the 21st Century* as one of the key contributors in the history of strategic management for his thought leadership in the field of strategic thinking.

Rich is the author of six books, including, *Deep Dive: The Proven Method for Building Strategy*, which has been described by the Director of Worldwide Operations for McDonalds as ". . . the most valuable book ever written on strategic thinking." His previous book, *Strategy for You: Building a Bridge to the Life You Want*, helps people apply the principles of business strategy to their overall lives and was the number-one bestselling book on Amazon.

Rich's innovative work in the field of strategic thinking has created dozens of proprietary offerings, including group workshops, assessments, books, mobile apps, workbooks, software, podcasts, videos, and one-to-one strategic counsel. A highly sought-after keynote speaker, Rich has spoken to leaders at world-class companies including Google, Intel, Emerson, and FedEx. His monthly e-publication, entitled *Strategic Thinker*, is read by thousands of business leaders and academicians around the world. Rich earned an MBA with Distinction from the Kellstadt Graduate School of Business at DePaul University and has completed advanced course work in strategy at the University of Chicago Booth School of Business and the Tuck School of Business at Dartmouth. He resides in Barrington Hills, Illinois.